AN AGORAPHOBIC'S
GUIDE TO HOLLYWOOD

To Tom & Steve,
Bonnie wanted you
to have this. Hope
you enjoy it.
Best wishes,
Darlene
Craviotto

AN AGORAPHOBIC'S GUIDE TO HOLLYWOOD

How Michael Jackson Got Me Out of the House

Darlene Craviotto

Front Door
Books

Published by

Front Door
Books

For Philip, who makes it easier for me to step out into the world.

For Cookie, who encourages me by reading my words.

For Marie, who inspires me with friendship, Dubonnet and Little Debbie moments.

Contents

This is a true story. Most of the meetings depicting Michael Jackson have been based on actual audiotapes made during those meetings. They were recorded at Michael's suggestion, and have never been shared publicly before. Some of the names of characters in this book have been changed to protect the privacy of individuals.

AN AGORAPHOBIC'S GUIDE TO HOLLYWOOD

ag•o•ra•pho•bia: abnormal fear of being helpless in an embarrassing or inescapable situation that is characterized especially by the avoidance of open or public places.

Merriam-Webster Dictionary

Introduction

I'm an agoraphobic.

It's taken me a lot of years to admit that. Nobody likes to confess they're different from the rest of the world. Especially when the world they live in is Hollywood. Oh sure, we all know that stars can be a little wacko, but that comes with the job. Bad press is still press, and any kind of press is good as long as they spell your name correctly. Superstars and their eccentricities have always been good for the box office.

But I'm a screenwriter, and there are different rules for those of us behind the scenes. Hollywood wants us normal because normal means no problems, and no problems means television shows and films come in on budget, and on time.

"Nobody needs to know about your little issue," my agent advised me when I finally had the courage to confide in him. I kept turning down lunch meetings (free food), pitch meetings (sometimes free food), studio screenings (free food and free booze), anything that took me out of my house. I was beginning to look a little strange. I had to tell him *something*.

"It's nobody's business but yours," he explained patiently, with a rare sensitivity seldom seen in agents.

I thanked him for being so understanding.

"Hello! They might stop hiring you!!!"

Now, he sounded like an agent.

We agreed never to talk about "my issue" again.

I continued to write. My career started to take off. I learned to work around the agoraphobia. I was always "too busy writing" to take lunches, dinner meetings, or studio interviews. I once met with a film producer for a 20th Century Fox project in my living room with its avocado green shag carpet and my grandmother's floral sofa. I was six months pregnant at the time, so it all seemed perfectly charming to the producer (a parent himself) who said he wished his wife had been so willing to "sit on the nest."

Once I started having babies, I had the best built-in excuses for staying home.

"I'm still breast feeding. I can't be away from the baby, or there's leakage. Can we do a phone conference?"

This worked especially well with nervous male producers. And since most producers who hired me were male, I was able to comfortably accommodate my agoraphobic needs for more years than breastfeeding is even possible. Sure, there were those occasional meetings I *had* to take to get the job. But since professional screenwriting assignments keep a writer busy (safely tucked away in her house) for at least six months, I could sweat my way through those occasional mandatory employment interviews. I always took a cab, made sure the meetings were brief ("I've got to get home to breastfeed"), and told the cabbie to take the fastest route home as possible. Once home, I would collapse, reach for a fast glass of Chardonnay, and vow to quit show business.

Somehow all of this worked.

And then one day Walt Disney Studios called me with a project that would change my life. They called it "Project M" so that no one would know about the true nature of the film. Why it was kept a secret I still don't understand. Except for a press leak early in the development stage, there was no further mention of the film at the time. It was to be a co-venture between Disney Studios and Amblin Entertainment, Steven Spielberg's film company. Steven was attached to direct, and equally as exciting, Michael Jackson would be its star. It was to be the film musical of *Peter Pan*. A blockbuster of a project and Disney wanted me to be the screenwriter.

No one has ever heard of it.

As a mater of fact, if you do a Google search, you won't find a thing on Project M. Although there is a brief mention in a Wikipedia entry that says Steven Spielberg was considering a musical of *Peter Pan* with Michael Jackson in the early 1980s but then reconsidered.

That's not exactly what happened.

This book tells the true story of Project M. It's a Hollywood tale, a behind-the-scenes look at show business: how we work, how we keep secrets, and ultimately how some of us are forced to grow up.

Peter Pan is all about growing up. It was my favorite story as a little girl; I loved Peter's adventures. His freedom and escapades are what excited me much more than Wendy's "stay-at-home" ways. True, she took flight with Peter, but she always ended up playing Mommy to the Lost Boys and cleaning up Peter's house. Not much fun to my seven-year-old sensibilities. My agoraphobic life certainly had taken a turn away from those carefree, fearless days of my youth. My adventures had become limited: I was housebound and surrounded by little children, domesticity, and my writing. I had turned into Wendy as a grown-up. But was this the kind of grown-up I really wanted to be?

Certainly not the housebound part.

As much as I loved *Peter Pan*, Michael Jackson loved the story even more. He named his ranch Neverland after J.M. Barrie's mystical island, and he filled his life with symbols and memorabilia from the imaginative tale about the boy who never grew up. Michael felt destined to play Peter. "I *am* Peter Pan," he would often say to me. And during Project M, in many ways, I became like Wendy to him.

When I first met Michael in 1990, the controversy that found him in later years was not there. But he was already being called "Wacko Jacko" by the gossip magazines. Bubbles the Chimp, plastic surgery, and sleeping in a hyperbaric chamber were listed as a few of his eccentricities. Okay, he had issues—but so did I.

And now I was going to be forced to face them.

Nobody told me when I first signed on for Project M that I'd have to meet privately with the biggest superstar in the world. I thought I'd take that one obligatory meeting, a little different this time because Spielberg, Jackson, and the head of the studio (gulp) were all in the room with me. But then I figured I'd speed back home in my cab, bolt back that one glass of medicinal Chardonnay, write the script in the safety of my home, get paid, and live happily ever after.

Life is not like the movies.

I didn't know it at the time, but this project wasn't going to be like any of the other projects I'd written. Working with Michael would not only be different, but I'd have to do something I hadn't been able to do for a long time.

Get out of the house.

This book is about how that happened.

1
Getting Past the Gates

Hollywood, 1990

Nobody living in L.A. ever takes a cab.

But there I was in the backseat of a red and white taxi with a Russian driver who could barely speak English. Not that it was a problem. We were in the film capital of the world, and Hollywood is spoken in every language. "Ivan" had no trouble understanding when he asked where I was going, and I told him Universal Studios.

"Da, Da, the tour!"

Uh, no. Not the tour, I tell him. I'd already spent three years in my 20s going to that tour, playing sheep dog to tourists as I pointed out Lana Turner's dressing room (as if anyone cared), and the Munster's House (as if anyone remembered) while wearing a red, white, and blue checker-board miniskirt. The tips I received I knew I was getting for my legs and not my oratory skills. The studio knew it too and built modesty gates to cover anything below our laps as we sat on the tram giving our spiel.

So much for tips.

"I have a meeting," I tell the driver. "You have to go in through the back gate." He looks into the rearview mirror, lifting his thick bushy eyebrows as he checks me out to see if I'm famous. In my mid-thirties, I still had the legs (somewhat more padded from having two kids and a sweet tooth) and long, silky hair (minus the split ends) left over from my tour guide days. The green-tinted aviatrix sunglasses I always wore added a certain glamorous show biz effect (I was blind as a bat without them), and I could see that the driver was trying to place me.

"Actress?"

"Not really."

"Yes, actress!!! Actress!!!" he insists.

I wasn't about to argue with a man behind the wheel of a speeding taxi going seventy. So I smiled and nodded and tried at least to pretend I was famous. Ivan looked thrilled to have me in his backseat as he turned the cab into the rear entrance of the Universal lot.

I had never come into the studio this way, and somehow it just felt so forbidden. This was the entrance they used for emergency vehicles and deliveries, not for legitimate meetings. Not for meetings that can change your life, that can buy you a house, and put your children through college.

"Just pull up to the guard's booth; I have to give my name," I instruct Ivan, and he pulls the cab over.

The uniformed guard approaches the driver's window, and bends down closer.

"Who are you here for?" he asks as his eyes search the back seat.

I take a breath.

"Steven Spielberg," I say.

Ivan gasps in the front seat, "Actress!!!!"

"I'm not an actress; I'm a writer," I explain. "A screenwriter."

The guard remains unimpressed as he checks a list on his clipboard.

"Name?"

I roll down the back window, preparing to spell it.

"Craviotto...C...R...A...V...I..."

"There's nothing listed."

"What? Wait. I haven't finished spelling it."

"There's nothing listed here."

"You want to check G? Maybe it's under G."

"Nothing."

He starts to go back inside his guard booth. In the front seat, Ivan turns around to stare at me in disappointment—I wasn't famous; I was just a screenwriter. Even worse, I was a screenwriter trying to sneak onto the lot.

Ivan looked so hurt and disillusioned.

"This is a mistake, okay? Could you check the list again?!" I call out to the guard.

Clearly, he's not listening because he isn't moving from the air-conditioned comfort of his tiny security booth.

"I have a meeting with Steven Spielberg!" I yell out to

him. "A lunch meeting with Steven Spielberg! At Amblin Entertainment, Steven Spielberg's production company!"

If I'm trying to impress the guard by overusing Steven's name, it's not working. I can tell by the way he's opening up his sack lunch that his investment in my plight is much less than his interest in whether his salami sandwich has mustard on it. I reach for the car handle and climb outside.

"Hey, you got to pay!" Ivan starts to swear in Russian, and the guard looks shocked to find me suddenly in his doorway.

"Could you call? Could you just please call Amblin?"

Ivan appears at my side, and Russian comes speeding out of his mouth.

"I'll pay!" I promise him. "Just wait, okay?"

After a few minutes of negotiation, the guard finally places a call to the Amblin offices. The receptionist seems to know nothing about the meeting or who I am. I frantically start naming names of every executive I've ever spoken to or met with at Amblin. But I'm terrible at names.

"Um...Debra...I think it's Debra...Yes! It's Debra...uh... Neu...something."

Where's my agent when I need him?!

The guard tightens his jaw; he looks ready to call for backup.

"Bettina Viviano!" I shout, suddenly remembering the one name I know because it's Italian, like mine. "Please call Bettina Viviano!!!"

I hold my breath as the guard puts down the salami sandwich and reaches for the phone. Above us, at the top of the Universal hill, I hear the voice of a tour guide in a parked tram stopped at the photo op point of the tour. The material was still the same: the guide pointed out Bob Hope's house, the water tower of Warner Brothers, and made the same tired joke about the brown smog covering the valley being a special effect. I still remembered the script perfectly. It would come in handy if this meeting killed my screenwriting career, and I needed to be rehired.

"Okay. You can go through."

I was stunned by the words. Five little words said with such indifference and with just a touch of mayo at the corner of his lips. They were words I had been waiting to hear for almost twenty years, giving me legitimacy and stature. I was about to take my first really Big Hollywood Meeting.

The guard pushed a button, and the electronic gate started to slowly rise. God Bless Bettina Viviano. I was finally going to meet Steven Spielberg...and someone else who was even bigger.

Ivan was all smiles.

2
Back Story

Hemingway's advice about writing is to write one true sentence. My advice is to just write anything. It doesn't matter if it's true, false, good, or bad. If you write it, it can be re-written. And in Hollywood chances are it'll be re-written by someone else. Just get anything down on paper because someone somewhere is going to find fault with it, think they can do better, or simply change it because it's their job. Knowing this not only helps you finish writing your scripts, but it should also help you say goodbye to them when they move on or end up gathering dust on a studio shelf somewhere.

You don't think about these realities when you're first hired. Anything seems possible when you're having celebratory dinners with agents, managers, parents, or lovers you want to impress. You consider yourself the most brilliant of screenwriters, certain that this project will either bring you the Oscar or at least permanent health benefits for the rest of your life. There's no better high than when the phone rings and your agent on the other end says, "They want you." It's the closest to sex you'll ever have with your clothes on.

In fact, writing a Hollywood screenplay is very much like dating. You meet. You fall in love. Everything about each other is magic. But pretty soon the criticisms begin: I don't like this about you; I don't like that. Change is expected, but of course it's never enough. And before you know it, you're out the door, shaking your head, "What the hell did I see in that person?" Of course, sometimes you luck out, and the relationship is productive: a film is born. But most times projects are like old soldiers (or the most painful of scars): they just fade away. You don't think about any of this when you're newly hired or when that first meeting comes around. All you know is that you're in love, and it will last forever. Life is good.

"Are you sitting down?" Depending on who asks you this will also depend if it's good news or bad. On this particular morning, the voice at the other end of the phone was my agent, Raymond. In his case, it could go either way.

"Disney wants you for a *huge* project," he announces after an obligatory dramatic pause. "Youwontevenbelievethis!" he squeals.

"I won't do animation," I tell him.

I had a good, solid movie of the week career, and my last script won an Emmy for outstanding television film. The last thing I wanted to do was to start writing cartoons. Not that I'm a snob (I love animation), but I just can't relate to characters that don't eat, pay bills, or go to the bathroom.

Disney started buzzing around me when I was nominated for the Emmy; the film I wrote went on to win, and the courtship heated up. The studio sent me a book they were considering, something they wanted to adapt as a feature film for Steven Spielberg to direct. It was to be a co-venture between Disney and Amblin at Universal. I liked the story a lot, but the studio was hesitant because it took place in Vietnam, and Disney felt Vietnam was too political.

"We're thinking it might work if we change it to the Korean Conflict," suggested one of the Disney executives, emphasizing "conflict" as clearly the more acceptable term when describing battles involving bloodshed. "The locale is still Asian, but people won't be put off by it." Heads nodded all around the room. "Steven's never done the Korean Conflict," one of the Amblin executives added hopefully. More nods. I saw a trend and decided to join it. "I could change the story to the Korean Conflict," I suggested. Of course I wasn't certain of this, but why buck the momentum especially when you don't have the job? I decided to dive in with full force, pitched them an opening, and sketched in some characters, conflict, and resolution. By the end of the day, my agent called and told me I had the job.

The final script on the project eventually was shelved; the official word was that Steven (who I never even had a chance to meet) had already done one war film with a boy in it, so this one was too similar. Why they never figured that out until paying my salary to write it, when all they had to do was read the novel it was based upon, I will never understand. Nor did I point it out to them, by the way, when they negotiated my deal.

But the good news was they loved, loved, loved my script. Jeffrey Katzenberg, who was head of Disney at the time, said it was the best script he had read in three years. Now we all know that Hollywood has been built on mounds of bullshit such as this. But I'm guessing he must have meant it, and Amblin's enthusiasm must have been genuine because here was my agent now on the phone telling me they wanted me for a huge project.

"It's not exactly animation," Raymond says, baiting me.

"I don't want to write *Beauty and the Beast*." (AUTHOR'S NOTE: That was probably a mistake).

"No, no, no, no, no! This is big! Big time! This will change your life!"

The suspense was killing me but my other phone line started to ring. With two young children, one in pre-school and the other in kindergarten, I had to pick it up.

"I'm putting you on hold, Raymond," I tell him quickly as I punched the other line.

"Wha…"

And he was gone.

"This is Howard Fein's office," a secretary announces at the other end. "Will you hold for Howard?"

I never have a chance to answer because Howard picks up.

"Are you sitting down?" Howard was the creative executive at Disney that I had been working with for the last year.

"Seriously, are you sitting?"

The light of my other line blinked as Raymond continued to hold.

"What do you love more than anything in the world?"

"My children," I tell him. "My husband," I quickly add. It was definitely a package deal.

"What *story*?" he emphasizes, forcing me to play this little game.

There were a lot of stories I loved. I was a big Katzankazis fan: *The Last Temptation of Christ. Zorba the Greek.* Not exactly Disney material. I could hear Howard sighing deeply at the other end of the phone while he waited for me to answer. He did this to me often when I was being slow to follow his lead.

"What property that will soon become public domain was made into a Broadway musical, a Disney animated classic, and a yearly Hallmark Special? Clap three times if you know the answer."

"Oh my God," I whisper.

Could it possibly be? Could it be the one kid's story that I was totally in love with? While waiting for a meeting to begin recently, I had confessed to Howard that there was one children's tale that had captivated my imagination from the very first time I had seen it when I was seven. I remember that he laughed at me as my eyes welled up with tears while talking about how special it was to me.

"Are you serious?" he'd asked.

"Very," I'd told him, reaching for the tissues on his desk. I was known for tearing up at anything that reminded me of being a child. I used to choke up when pointing out the "Leave It to Beaver" house on the Universal tour.

"I wouldn't tell that to too many people," Howard had advised. "At least not in Hollywood."

"I don't," I'd admitted. "You brought it up, not me."

I had wondered at the time why *was* he bringing it up.

"I'm glad you told me," he had said, in his own cryptic kind of way. Replaying that scene now it all suddenly started to make sense.

"*Peter Pan*?" I ask, incredulously.

"It's not just *Peter Pan*. There's more."

Peter Pan was more than enough. How could there be more?

"Do you know who wants desperately to play Peter?"

I can hardly hear what he's saying as my ears start ringing in excitement.

"Who's the biggest star you can think of?"

A woman had always played the role onstage; Mary Martin had starred as Peter on Broadway and later Sandy Duncan and Cathy Rigby. I searched through a mental list of actresses that were currently big film stars.

"Meg Ryan?" I ask.

"Don't insult me!"

"Meryl Streep, Barbra Streisand, Bette Midler, Sally Field…"

He stops me with one name.

"Michael Jackson."

I can't speak. My mouth refuses to form words.

"Hello?" Howard says, raising his voice.

It was 1990, and Michael Jackson was the most well-known and well-loved international pop star. *Thriller* was the best-selling album ever—in the entire history of recorded music. Since he had played the Scarecrow in the film version of *The Wiz*, Hollywood had been trying to reel Michael in for more acting roles. His performances in the videos *Billie Jean*, *Beat It*, and *Thriller* only whetted Hollywood's desire to find a starring vehicle for him. Michael was at the pinnacle of his success, and if Disney could sign him to the right vehicle, this could make the studio a lot of money.

"Michael Jackson wants to play Peter Pan?" I say slowly, making sure I understood exactly what Howard was telling me.

"And Steven is going to direct it," he adds.

"Ste..Ste…Steven?"

"Did you have a stroke?" Howard asks impatiently. "Why are you not following this?"

A Steven Spielberg production starring Michael Jackson. Written by me?! Now I really needed to sit down. No, actually what I needed was a large anything alcoholic.

"We've been putting this together for the last few months. Why do you think I asked you about *Peter Pan* at that story meeting? Steven loved your script. Jeffrey loved your script. Steven loves Michael's talents. Michael loves *Peter Pan*. Disney owns *Peter Pan*. The *Peter Pan* story goes public domain this year, and if we don't put something together somebody else will."

He waits for me to say something.

"Are you still with me?

"I'm not sure … How do I … Why do you … ?"

He didn't want to wait for my brain to start functioning again; he had to move on.

"You're the right writer at the right time. Don't question it. A simple thank you will do."

"Thank you," I say, finally making some sense.

"We'll set up a meeting, and I'll call you."

"Ok, fine. Any time!"

"One more thing," he adds. "You can't tell anyone about this. It's a top secret project absolutely no one can know about." And then he says forcefully, "If it leaks out, we'll deny it. And the project goes away."

The phone went dead before I could ask him why.

The biggest job of my life, and I wasn't allowed to tell anyone I had it.

I doubted my agent would be thrilled to hear this.

3
"Project M"

They called it "Project M."

"It sounds like something for hemorrhoids," says Raymond over Thai food at Bangkok One. It was our official congratulatory lunch date, and we were eating at the only restaurant that felt comfortable to me. It was just two blocks away (two long blocks) from my apartment, and Raymond had picked me up in a Jaguar, no questions asked.

"That's Preparation H, not M," I inform him. "Project M sounds more like a military mission. Like we're building a bomb at Las Cruces."

"Please don't say bomb!" Raymond says nervously, reaching for the saltshaker, and tossing salt over his shoulder for luck. "Don't jinx this, please!"

"Well, whatever it's called, we can't talk about it."

"What does *that* mean?"

"Not officially we can't. Howard says it's top secret, and he doesn't want it to get around town."

"How am I supposed to use a project that sounds like a

CIA assignment to get you more work?"

"Why do I need more work? I just got hired."

"Don't get cocky."

I knew he wouldn't be thrilled about this.

Raymond was young and high-strung: the new kid on the block. I had inherited him from the woman whose name graced the letterhead of the boutique agency that had represented me since I had retired from acting/tour guiding and started writing. The Leanne Green Agency had signed me twelve years earlier as their first client. No, correct that, actually Leanne's ex-husband had been her first client. A New York short story writer who hated Hollywood, he only moved to L.A. to be close to his son who Leanne had conveniently whisked away to Tinseltown. Smart move on Leanne's part because Leo Green followed after her and ended up as one of television's premiere creators of primetime serial dramas. Leo made big money; Leanne assumed I'd do the same.

But I had other ideas: I only wanted to write films. I took my chances freelancing (i.e., making less money) and let the other clients bankroll Leanne's Hollywood Hills lifestyle by producing and creating television series. Leanne got bored; enter Raymond, a 26-year-old Valley College graduate who loved show tunes, Warner Brothers post war films, and my writing. I wanted to work in features, and Raymond was more than happy to labor night and day for that to happen. Exit Leanne, hello Raymond. With Leanne's blessing, Raymond took over the reins of my career, and I had my first feature assignment within a year.

Now we were poised to really crack the town open: Project M was set to be my breakout feature film project. If only we could tell people I was writing it.

"What does Leanne say about this?" I ask.

"She's in Paris for a week taking Cordon Bleu cooking lessons. She's in a different time zone."

"That explains the Jaguar."

"Shh! Please don't tell her I borrowed it."

The restaurant was starting to fill up with the lunch crowd, and my nerves were beginning to kick in. I was ready to leave, but Raymond was just settling in.

"You can bet your firstborn it wasn't Disney's idea to keep this top secret," Raymond says as he slides more Pad Thai onto his plate. "They'd take out a billboard on Sunset, if it was up to them. This is all Wacko Jacko. He's the one who wants this top secret." Reaching for the chili sauce, he covers his noodles with it while he picks out the cilantro leaves, discarding them neatly on an extra napkin. "Amblin has their confidentiality agreements, and that whole nuttiness, but this is just over the top." He starts to pick out the peanuts from another dish and add them to his noodles. "The kid is nuts!"

"The kid is four years older than you are."

"He's still nuts," Raymond lowers his voice, confidentially, "He sleeps with a chimp named Bubbles. Did you know that?!"

I nod. To each his own. This was Hollywood, for Pete's Sake, not Des Moines, Iowa.

"*And* he owns a hyperbaric chamber that he takes naps in so he won't age. Tell me that isn't creepy. Tell me that isn't strange."

"My mother reads the *National Enquirer* too, Raymond."

"I do not read the *Enquirer*!" I absolutely do not!"

I give him a look. And he confesses.

"My Bubbe in Encino told me. She reads them, not me!"

"I'm not going to judge someone's mental health who I haven't even met yet. Besides, most of those stories are made up," I insist.

Raymond loved to gossip, and most times I didn't mind listening. But this just felt wrong. I was going to be creating a major role for Michael Jackson, and I didn't see how hearing about his eccentricities, real or not, could help me shape the character of Peter Pan. If anything probably the less I knew about Michael, the better.

"They want you to work with him."

"Who?"

"The. Person. Who. Can't. Be. Named," he says as though we were playing Jeopardy and that was the category. Leaning across the table, he whispers, "Michael!"

"What do you mean … work with him?"

"That's part of the deal. You and Michael side by side, working on the story together."

The restaurant was getting warmer. I reached for my water.

"Does this involve leaving my house?" I ask, trying to disguise the terror lurking underneath the words.

"Of course!"

My heart started to pound and not in a good way.

The last thing I wanted to do was leave my house, even if it meant working with Michael Jackson. It's not that I loved staying home so much; it's just that I had this little problem.

Panic attacks.

I was afraid to leave the house because of them.

I didn't always have them. Certainly, as a tour guide I was fearless in front of the tourists. I'd been trained as an actress, and I was used to performing onstage. Getting out of my house had never been a problem before. When I was 19, I traveled down the coast from my hometown in Santa Barbara, transferring to UCLA as an excuse I gave to my parents for moving to Hollywood. I wanted to be an actress. Not that Hollywood cared. It took me seven years to finally get my Screen Actors Guild card and to become a professional. My acting career was just getting started.

And then, I made a mistake.

The biggest mistake in my life.

I let someone drive me home who shouldn't have been behind the wheel. Speeding along Sunset Blvd. at midnight, our car tried to perform the impossible task of occupying the same space at 40 mph as an already parked vehicle. The impact threw me forward, and it wasn't until the next day, when a friend went to look at the car, returning pale and shaken, that I learned my face had gone through the windshield. I should have been able to guess this from the large cut across my eyebrow (bleeding profusely and in need of a plastic surgeon) and the glass that was dug out from my cornea in the E.R. But at the time my only real concern was whether or not I'd be able to appear in front of a camera in less than a week.

After taking seven years to get into the acting union, I had finally gotten my first break co-starring in a feature film. My big scene was coming up in a few days, and that meant a close-up. The last thing you want to do before having your final close-up is to smash the windshield of your 1967 Chevy Malibu into your face. The plastic surgeon assured me that my wounds would heal up eventually but not before the cameras were scheduled to roll. My perfect close-up ended up with me looking like Rocky Balboa at the end of any one of the first three *Rockys*. Not the best way for an actress to build a career.

But it wasn't just my face that was injured in that accident. Suddenly, I became afraid to leave the house. I'd find myself breaking out in a cold sweat anywhere I'd go. The grocery store seemed overwhelming, standing in line at the bank felt endless until my heart would start racing, and I'd have to bolt. Forget about going anywhere like a mall, a theatre, or sporting event where there might be hundreds or (God forbid) thousands of people. My mind would fog up just at the thought of it, and I'd find myself walking around in a daze.

So I simply stayed home.

When you're housebound, it's amazing how much time you have on your hands. I filled it with writing. If I couldn't go outside and experience life at least I could live it in my imagination. I started to write scripts. When I finished one, I'd begin another. When that was done, I'd try my hand at one more. A friend asked if he could read one of my scripts. He liked it and gave it to another friend who was a secretary at Warner Brothers. She liked it and gave it to another friend, an intern working for a director. The intern liked it, came over for drinks, made a pass (I passed), and asked if he could give my script to a friend who was a new agent from New York. Enter Leanne. I signed with her the following week; she sent my script out as a writing sample. I learned how to take cabs, and I was a professional screenwriter in less than a year.

All because I never left the house.

The wonderful thing about being a writer is that no one cares if you ever leave the house. As a matter of fact, producers like it that way. The more time spent indoors, the faster you can crank out the work. The first script I was paid to write, I finished in one week. As I turned it in, the story editor stared at me in disbelief. Taking me off to the side for privacy, he said, "Don't ever do this again. Just put it in a drawer and make us wait." I got the message: if you finish it in a week, they expect you to write every script that quickly. I followed his advice, and I kept getting hired. Somewhere along the way I managed to find myself a life.

Thanks to Leanne.

"Leo wants you to be executive story editor for his new show," she had announced between bites of chicken and cashews at Bangkok One. This was pre-Raymond when Leanne was still in the picture, having high hopes for me making big bucks in television.

"Could I do that at home?" I had asked. It seemed like a perfectly rational question to me, so I didn't understand why she would be laughing.

"You need to stop that," she said.

"Stop what?"

"That thing you're doing. It's not good."

"I'm working. I'm making money. I don't see a problem."

"You don't have a life."

"I have my writing."

"It's not a life. You need to take this job, get out of the house, get yourself a life, a nice guy. A husband, even."

I liked Leanne when she was acting like a nice Jewish mother.

She must have slipped something into my Thai ice tea because I surprised myself and took the job. I even tried driving again (my last official attempt while living within the greater Los Angeles area), traveling barely the speed limit all the way from West Hollywood to Burbank. And you know something? I did meet a nice guy, a nice Jewish guy named David.

Leanne was so proud.

I married David, giving up my office staff job (and driving) to return to freelance screenwriting. Also, to go back to my home sweet home where I now had a husband to keep me company, and I couldn't care less if we ever went out

again. I probably would have stayed in my house forever, like
Rapunsel in her tower, except for one thing: kids.

Jacob was born, and then Kathryn three and half years
later. Being a Mommy that doesn't drive or like to leave her
house can seriously cramp your kid's social life. It was one
thing for me to stay home, that was my own choice. But my
children needed other kids to play with and schools to attend.
David acted as chauffeur on the weekends, but during the
week we needed extra help. We hired a nanny that had a car.
And I stayed in the house and just kept writing.

Until this lunch when Raymond said I had to meet with
Michael Jackson.

"How many times?" I carefully ask.

"How many...?"

"Times would we have to meet?"

"As many times as it takes. This is Michael Jackson we're
talking about!" Raymond says, confused by the question.

I could feel the blood pounding in my ears as I tried hard
not to notice my breathing. Do your lungs stop working if
you're aware of them? What happens if your heart just stops,
do you feel it? These were questions I didn't need to be asking
myself at the moment as I glanced over at the door to the restaurant, looking for the fastest way I could bolt out of there.
This is why I didn't take lunch meetings or any other kind of
meetings. This is why I didn't like going out at all.

"You can do this, right?" Raymond asks, hesitantly, as he
watches me remove my jacket, unbutton the top button of my

blouse, slip my sunglasses on, and retreat into a corner of the booth. Although we hadn't formally talked about my "little problem," he knew I had one.

"This'll be good for you---It'll be fun! It'll get you out of the house!"

That's what I was afraid of.

"You can *do* this, Darlene," Raymond insists, sounding like a motivational speaker. And then adds quickly, "You haven't told anybody about this, this little thing you have, right?"

I shake my head.

It was my own little secret, and one I tried desperately to keep to myself.

"Good! No one in the business needs to know this," he says, signaling for the check. "I don't care what you tell your friends, but in this town that's a sick puppy we don't talk about. Agreed?"

"Agreed," I say, closing my eyes, and trying desperately not to black out.

I could feel myself retreating into my own version of Neverland where restaurants didn't exist or agents or any kind of phobias whatsoever. There in that corner of the booth, I pretended I was somewhere else and hoped like hell that would get me through the rest of this lunch. If I could do it here, maybe it would even work with Michael.

"Don't worry about a thing!" Raymond assures me. "Michael's going to love you!" he says proudly, reaching over for the check. "You're just as weird as he is!"

Somehow that wasn't reassuring.

4
A Really Big Meeting

Visiting Amblin Entertainment on the Universal Studio lot was just like taking a vacation. Named after Steven Spielberg's student film, *Amblin'*, the production complex was tucked away in a back corner of the studio, far away from the tourist crowded trams. It was built to look exactly like a Southwestern hacienda made of earthen toned adobe and surrounded by brilliant bougainvillea, lush greenery, and towering palms.

Steven was raised in Scottsdale, Arizona and his production offices were built to reflect a Spanish influence. From the terra cotta clay floor tiles throughout the entire building to the interior courtyard of fruit trees and vegetable gardens, it was a lavish paradise, a momentary respite from the smoggy San Fernando Valley in which it was built.

And what better place than a movie studio to invent such a vision of another time, another place, another reality? The Amblin Entertainment compound blended in cohesively with the other facades on the backlot: a half block away from a street that looked like Midwest America, two blocks from a cobblestoned European village, and three blocks from the brownstones of New York. None of this was real of course, and none of the buildings had more than one or two walls. Amblin Entertainment was the exception—a real-life building in the middle of make-believe.

Ivan-the-cabbie had never seen anything like this before. He mumbled softly in Russian, and his eyes widened as he drove the taxi through the elaborate wooden gates of the outside adobe walls surrounding the complex. A security guard with a walkie-talkie met us and signaled Ivan to stop. He was a huge, NFL-sized man dressed in chinos and a blue blazer.

"Can I help you?"

Ivan nervously pointed to the back seat, expecting another problem I guess, and I leaned forward to say my name. The security man repeated it (mispronouncing it) into his walkie-talkie, and I held my breath, hoping this time I was on some secret list somewhere that made me special. A voice crackled back in acknowledgement, and we were waved forward.

Into film history, I hoped.

Howard, the Disney executive who had hired me for this project, was waiting impatiently at the front entrance of the building.

"Where have you been?!"

"They wouldn't let me on the lot!" I tell him as he whisks me through the front doors.

"You're making that up," he says guiding me through the foyer.

"I'm not! Ask my driver."

"Driver? What driver?!" We were heading into forbidden territory. Heeding my agent's advice, I didn't want to get into it. Not here. Not now.

"I took a cab," I reluctantly mumble, hoping he doesn't ask for more of an explanation.

"Nobody takes a cab in L.A!" He looks at me in shock. "Why on earth would you take a cab?"

I was saved by Jeffrey Katzenberg, President of Disney Films, who appeared almost on cue as we took a short cut through the interior courtyard.

"Are we doing this?!" he asks, with just a touch of impatience.

"Right now," Howard tells him, quickly introducing me as we move a little faster back into the building and down a hallway to Steven's private dining room.

"Loved the script, Diane." Jeffrey tells me, never slowing his step.

"Thank you," I say, just trying to keep up, and not correcting him. If the head of the studio wanted to change my name to "Diane," well, at least for that meeting I'd be "Diane."

We arrived at Steven's private dining room, and the thick ornately-carved wooden doors opened almost like magic. We stepped inside, the three of us, and there sat Steven Spielberg at the head of a long wooden dining table set for lunch. He rose to meet us, his hand outstretched, and I smiled, said hello, and tried like hell not to pass out at his feet. There are those times in your life when you just want to freeze the moment and keep it forever. This was one of those times. I hadn't felt this excited about meeting someone since I first met my two babies after giving birth. But other than childbirth, there was nothing that could possibly top this excitement of meeting Steven Spielberg.

"Have you met Michael yet?"

Unless it was meeting Michael Jackson.

Steven turned and gestured across the table, and there he sat. His eyes are what I noticed first; they were the most stunning-looking eyes I've ever seen on a man. Large in shape and the deepest of brown, they pulled you in, almost hypnotically, and kept your attention. It was impossible not to stare at this man. I've often wondered if he was wearing eyeliner that day; his eyes were so beautifully shaped and defined. But in later meetings when it was just the two of us, and no need to be the star, those eyes still were stunning: still captured you and pulled you into his world.

We smiled at each other across the table and said hello quietly. I found it curious that he didn't rise and shake my hand, like Steven had and Jeffrey too. At first, I had assumed that Michael thought he didn't have to stand. He was famous, and famous people are used to being privileged. But later, after I spent time with him, I realized that something else had kept him seated that day: he was just too shy to stand.

The meeting began, and it was just like any other. Hollywood meetings are built around chitchat. Participating in witty repartee, consisting of the right amount of gossip and the most politically correct opinions, is almost as important in getting hired in the film industry as your talent. I wasn't good at it. And judging by Michael's silence, he wasn't good at it either.

Chitchat begins the moment we are all seated around the table. Michael and I face each other with Howard at my side and Jeffrey at Steven's; Steven, of course, sits at the head of the table. There's a murmuring of who's drinking what, while a young Amblin intern takes orders.

"I'll have a coke," Steven says and then adds, "with chocolate. I'll have a chocolate coke." This pretty much stops everyone in the room and thus begins the chitchat portion of the meeting.

"A chocolate coke?!" Jeffrey asks, incredulously.

The Amblin intern is stopped in his tracks. Obviously, he's new and not sure what this involves.

"A chocolate…I'm sorry…A coke that's chocolate. It's chocolate?" he sputters.

"Have you got some chocolate?" Steven asks him, patiently. "Hershey's, maybe? You take the coke, and you put some chocolate in it."

"How much do I put in?" the intern asks, hoping like hell not to blow this. They didn't teach him these things at USC Film School.

"Just a little. Not a lot. But enough," Steven tells him, trying to be a good mentor.

The intern still looks lost.

"You know, just bring me the syrup; I'll do it myself," Steven says, gently dismissing him with a smile.

"A chocolate coke?!" Jeffrey says again. "Are you joking?"

"Didn't you ever drink chocolate cokes?"

"There's two kinds of cokes—cherry cokes, and vanilla," Jeffrey recites, as though it were litany.

"You gotta have a chocolate coke, chocolate's the best!" Steven announces with great finality. "With Bosco. Hersheys is good, but Bosco's the best."

"Sounds like a jingle," Howard adds.

"I remember Bosco," I say in a most confident voice. Having pitched in my one essential comment, I was now able to do what I did best: listen and observe. And so for the next ten minutes I watched Jeffrey, Howard, and Steven debate the merits of chocolate cokes: the best chocolate to use in making chocolate cokes, the precise amount of chocolate to use (this while watching Steven make his own chocolate coke), whether chocolate cokes are East Coast or West Coast in derivation, other potential flavors for flavored cokes, and a brief comparison between chocolate cokes and egg creams.

Michael sat across from me, watching the proceedings with a smile. He followed the exchange of banter, enjoying it, and laughing at times. But from a distance. When he finally did speak, it was with a kind of genuine softness, almost forcing you to lean a little forward to hear him. I hadn't expected Michael to be this timid and bashful. Someone who looked totally at home in front of an audience of thousands seemed oddly awkward here in this private dining room with only four other people. I knew the look; I recognized the discomfort. Settled back in his chair, Michael appeared as uncomfortable as I felt. In a room full of adults, we were clearly two kids who were in desperate need of a children's table.

When lunch was served (a Southwestern chicken with a fruit salsa), Michael didn't touch his food. Instead, he sipped occasionally at an orange colored liquid in a plastic container in front of him. I wondered what it was: Gatorade? MacDonald's orange soda? Or some special concoction of vitamins and minerals made especially for Michael? Steven noticed it too, and at one point said to him, "You better eat, Mike. You're going to need all your strength for this project." "Oh, I will," Michael had assured him. "I'll be ready."

It was impossible not to watch Michael, to study him throughout the lunch. He was directly across from me—a mere six feet, and I could perceive a palpable vulnerability that at times rivaled my own, replacing my self-conscious anxiety with an almost maternal concern for him.

"Are you ready to fly?" Steven asks, jump-starting the meeting into the reason why we were all in the room. "Ready to strap on the harness and take flight, Mike?"

"Oh yes!" Michael says, breathlessly.

"It's the one thing man wants more than anything in the

world," Steven begins, officially kicking off the project and turning the meeting away from chitchat to creative musings. "The one universal desire that all people have is to be able to fly. I have dreams all the time, and I'm flying in them. It's the one thing I'd give everything up for: the ability to fly."

"I have those dreams too!" Michael says, leaning forward, and for the first time seeming engaged and no longer uncomfortable.

"That's why this story has been around so long, and it means so much to people. It touches on that universal quest for flight," Steven explains.

"Well, we do have airplanes," says Jeffrey, ever the pragmatist.

"Not the same," Steven insists. "Not like spreading your wings and taking flight with unlimited 360 degree views. Can you imagine what that must feel like? What a rush that would be? We only know that through our dreams. But it can't be duplicated in real life. The person who comes up with a way to make man fly...like that? Like a bird? There's not enough money in the world to pay for that experience, that kind of power. That sense of total freedom in flight."

Damn. Spielberg was good. I was hooked. It wasn't so much what he was saying that impressed me, but the fact that it was Steven Spielberg who was saying it. The brilliance wasn't in his words, but in the surety and authority that came with them. As Steven talked on and on about the excitement in *Peter Pan*, how it had never been translated to the screen before, my imagination filled in the blanks. All of his movies flashed before me with that spectacular, bigger-than-life Spielberg touch. Yes, we had all seen *Peter Pan* done before, Steven was suggesting, but not like this, not with him at the helm to unleash the visual splendor. This would be the ultimate cinematic event.

"The timing wasn't right before to make a *Peter Pan* movie," Michael assures Steven, in a soft but certain tone of voice. "It takes *all* the right ingredients at the right time to come together."

It was a gentle nudge to the director for a star's equal billing.

Michael was 32, at the peak of his career and popularity, and he had this wonderful androgynous look, like a young boy not yet forced into manhood. No man had ever played the role of Peter Pan before, and there wasn't another actor I could think of who could capture the child-like enthusiasm, spirit of mischief, and simple earnestness of Peter Pan. No other actor than Michael. He was as equally important as the director in this cinematic event. And Michael wanted it clear that Steven knew that.

"Are you sure you want to do this," Steven teases. "You're sure you're committed to it?"

"Absolutely!" Michael says, his enthusiasm clearly evident in the large grin on his face.

"We're not going to lose you to some world tour…?"

"This is a dream of mine," Michael assures him.

"...or back to back albums?"

"I want to be Peter!"

"It's going to be a lot of work, a lot of commitment," Steven says, seriously.

Michael nods his head. "I'm ready to do this. I've been waiting my whole life."

Steven was like a father about to loan the car keys to his teenage son, but making sure the kid could handle the responsibilities. He needed to hear the right answers from the star, and so far Michael's enthusiasm was encouraging to him. It made him press on, ever the competent director, the man always at the helm; he shared his thoughts about Peter and Hook and all of the characters. He would paint a cinematic nirvana called Neverland, a place we hadn't seen on film before. Populating it in a way that had never been attempted, or imagined even by J.M. Barrie himself. Everything would be filtered through the Steven Spielberg lens: the pirates, the Jolly Roger ship (oh what a set that would be–the biggest and best pirate ship in all of film history), and the flying scenes with the best special effects, infusing a reality never portrayed in *Peter Pan* before.

I sat there, slack-jawed, watching in amazement as Steven worked his magic. I wished I had brought my tape recorder. It was something I always did with story meetings to help me remember executive notes and script beats. Usually I was so nervous just getting to the meetings I needed to record them so I could remember everything we had discussed. It hadn't seemed appropriate to tape a lunch meeting, but here was Steven Spielberg on a creative roll, and I was totally unprepared. This is why I never liked to take lunch meetings. I can't eat and be creative at the same time. It has something to do with the circulation rushing to my stomach and not my brain. I wasn't prepared at the moment to be brilliant. Or even competent.

"Did you have some ideas, Darlene?"

Oh please, don't let that be Steven asking. But it was.

Let me take this moment to say that until the contracts have been signed, the ink dried, a commencement check received (with your name spelled correctly), and deposited (without bouncing), no deal is ever certain. And at this point in time, my agent was still negotiating monies. If I blew this meeting, I could be dropped from the project.

"I'd like to read J.M. Barrie's novel first," I say, carefully. "We should go to the source material. That's where we'll find our answers."

I didn't know if it was the correct thing to say, but it was what I believed. J.M. Barrie's *Peter Pan* was responsible for getting the group of us there in that dining room. Something about his writing spoke to us, made us fall in love with the story and the people in it; and in Disney's case, it had made the studio a lot of money. The least we could do was to go to Barrie's words first, and see where they would guide us. Whether the others in the room agreed with me, I wasn't sure.

As I looked around at everyone, I couldn't get a read: first to Steven, then to Jeffrey, and finally to Howard at my side.

Not one of them seemed particularly impressed or even sure I was the right writer in the room. I wasn't sure at that moment either. Until I looked across the table and saw Michael smiling gently at me, and his smile said it all.

Welcome to Neverland.

5
The Night of the Grammys

Nothing is done quickly in Hollywood.

Several months had passed since Disney first contacted me about the *Peter Pan* project, and now we were all waiting for Michael's schedule to free up. He was in the middle of making a new album called *Dangerous*, and he was working long hours at a recording studio.

"Michael can meet with you at 9," I am told in a phone call on a Monday for a Wednesday meeting.

For a working Mom with two little kids under six, it was short notice.

"We drop the kids off at school at 9," I start to explain. "But I could ask my nanny to come in earlier."

"P.M."

"Excuse me?"

"Michael can only meet with you at night," says Stella, the woman who seems to be in charge of running Michael's life. "He has a very full schedule, and there's no time during the day we can squeeze this in."

"9 p.m. is fine," I lie.

9 p.m. was just after the kids' bath time (when I ended up soaked), followed by putting them to bed (wishful thinking), and lying down to read to them (when I usually fell asleep). 9 p.m. was my glass of Chardonnay and Twix bar hour when I celebrated being off duty. Now I was being asked to crank up my energy and be creative. I wasn't exactly thrilled at the idea, and more importantly, I wasn't even sure I could stay awake. But this was a meeting with Michael Jackson, somehow I had to make this work. So I said yes and booked a sitter.

Stella called me late in the afternoon the day before the meeting.

"Michael wants to push up the meeting to 6 p.m."

No problem, I again lie, hoping the sitter will be as flexible.

She isn't.

I beg, I plead, I promise autographed photos from Michael, but she has a life (and kids) too, and she's unavailable.

Unless you're on your deathbed, you don't cancel meetings in Hollywood, and even if you are at death's door, you better be willing to at least take a conference call. There aren't that many women screenwriters in the business, and the last thing any one of us wants to do is give the town another reason not to hire us. ("Her sitter list is thin, we better get Aaron Sorkin.") This means that if you're a mom, you better know the names and whereabouts of every nanny, housekeeper, or teenage girl that lives within a Los Angeles zip code.

By the time my husband got home from work that night, I was at the end of my sitter list, and my wits.

"I'll watch the kids," said David, figuring how hard could it be?

Our kids proceeded to show him.

That night, Kathryn, our two year old, started coughing at bedtime. By the next day, she had double ear infections and threw up five times before lunch. To make matters worse, our five year old, Jacob, came down with a fever by dinnertime.

As my husband walked through the front door, ready for his babysitting assignment, I was doling out doses of baby Tylenol, pink ampicillin, and cherry popsicles for dinner.

"I'll be back before the next dose of Tylenol!" I say, handing him the thermometer, and *Goodnight, Moon.*

"Which is when?!" he asks, hoping it'll be soon.

"I have to be out of there by 8 because Michael has to watch the Grammys," I announce, trying not to sound too smug for being on a first name basis with Michael Jackson.

"Can't he work regular hours like everyone else?"

This is show biz, I remind my husband, who is an actor, and should know better. But he's in between jobs at the moment and not too happy knowing Michael's got an acting gig, and he doesn't. Plus, he isn't exactly thrilled with my new working hours or having to play Mr. Mom to two vomiting, bad-tempered kids.

"How are you getting there?" David asks, not aware of the usual cab horn blaring impatiently outside. Almost on cue, there is a knock at the door, and I open it to reveal a chauffeur dressed all in black.

A sleek, shiny-new Town Car waits in our driveway like a vision out of some modern-day fairy tale. The driver's name is Jerry, and he looks like every tram driver who ever drove me as a tour guide. A friendly Teamster with a buzz cut, he likes to talk, and it takes my mind off where I'm going, and who I'll be meeting with when I get there.

"I usually drive Steven," Jerry says to me as I melt into the smooth leather backseat. "He prefers this to the limousine."

Of course, don't we all?

"I usually take cabs," I say, embarrassed that a perfectly good Ford Taurus is sitting in our driveway, and I can't drive it. I only hope he doesn't ask me why.

"You must really rate to get Steven's car."

I hadn't asked for this; it was my agent's little surprise.

"I put it in your contract," Raymond had said proudly the day he called me to let me know he had closed the deal. "They have to provide a car and a driver to take you to all of your meetings."

"Did you tell them I have a problem with driving, and leaving the house?"

"Shhh! I don't know what you're talking about. Everybody drives in L.A."

"What did you tell them?"

"That you were from New York. Nobody drives in Manhattan!"

I could get used to this type of transportation.

We drove down Santa Monica Blvd. towards Beverly Hills, heading into Westwood and to a place Stella had called "The Hideaway." It was Michael's special...well, hideaway: a secret place where he could escape and keep the world at a distance. It was a penthouse located in a building off Wilshire Blvd. that few people knew about or ever saw.

"Michael goes there at nights after he's been in the studio recording all day," Stella had told me. "It's very private. He doesn't let many people go there. It's his secret hideout–somewhere he can unwind, and just be on his own. You won't be bothered there; there won't be any interruptions."

Better than working at my place, I guess. We lived in West Hollywood where male hustlers hung out at the end of our street, and female prostitutes hustled three blocks in the opposite direction. Our nights were punctuated by the thumping of chopper blades as a police helicopter buzzed our neighborhood, accompanied by a bullhorn: "To the perpetrators: Come out with your hands up or we'll release the dogs!"

No wonder I never wanted to leave the house.

"You have to be out of the Hideaway by 8, no exceptions!" Stella had instructed. "Michael has to watch the Grammy's, and he can't be interrupted."

This sounded like a deal breaker, and I didn't want to risk the wrath of Stella by blowing it. Inside the Town Car, I checked my watch to coordinate the time and suddenly noticed I wasn't wearing it. I must have forgotten to put it on in my hurry to get out of the house.

"I have to be picked up before 8," I tell Jerry, trying not to panic. "I don't have a watch, so can you honk really loudly or something?"

Jerry laughs and slips his watch off his wrist. Handing it back to me, "This'll probably work better."

"Really? You don't mind?"

"Be my guest," he says with a smile. "I don't think you'd hear me honking," he adds as he pulls off of Wilshire and into a circular driveway in front of the tallest high rise on the street.

A uniformed doorman stands waiting as we pull up and stop. Jerry points to the top of the building. "Michael's in the penthouse all the way up on the 24th floor." Winking, he adds, "I'll be here when you need me."

Everything slows down as my nerves begin to kick in. Like a scene shot in slow motion, people seem to be moving in half-time, and their words are low and guttural.

The doorman opens up the car door for me, as Jerry announces, "She's here to see Mr. Jackson." A phone call is placed upstairs to the penthouse. "Mr. Jackson says to send you right up." The doorman smiles, and with a tip of his hat, I'm granted an entrance.

I float into the building, hoping no one will wake me on my way.

The elevator takes forever, and with each floor my heart pounds harder. I reach the 24th floor and glide my way down a hallway to the penthouse door. I knock, and a voice inside calls out to me to come in. I try the doorknob, and I'm surprised to find it unlocked. There are no bodyguards, or security people; I wonder if I have the correct apartment. Cautiously, I step inside.

As soon as I enter, I know I have the right place. Faces of child stars look down from the walls—Shirley Temple, in black and white, has the most prominent position, and she stares down at me, watching as I move deeper into the living room.

Toys are scattered all around—G.I. Joe original dolls (the big sized ones from the 1960s) and a toy jeep sit on the living room floor. There are plexiglass enclosed *Star Wars* models sitting in the middle of the room, and a life-size KFC Colonel Sanders statue holding a ceramic bucket of his fried chicken (also ceramic) leaning against a wall. An antique Coca-Cola machine stands guard next to the entrance of the kitchen. The sparse living room (large in size) is filled with nondescript furniture that looks as though it's been rented. This place seems more like a bachelor pad than a star's home.

I sit on the couch in the living room and wait for what feels like forever. No one else is around; there are no handlers, assistants, or managers. It's just me and the life-like Colonel Sanders and the hum of the Coca-Cola machine. I am wearing a Laura Ashley print with a Peter Pan collar and Mary Jane pumps with ankle socks. I'm sure I must look exactly like Wendy.

I hear him before I see him.

"Do you want anything, Darlene?" he calls out to me.

I'm thrilled he remembers my name.

"Something to drink?" he asks, deep inside the kitchen.

"No, I'm fine!" I'm somehow able to find the words to call back.

He appears with a pitcher of ice water and a glass.

"There's some sodas in there too," he tells me and I watch as he makes himself comfortable, setting up the pitcher, and taking a seat in an armchair across from me. He does all this just so naturally. As though he's not aware that he's the King of Pop or the fantasy of millions all over the world. Dressed in black slacks, a buttoned red shirt (untucked), and black loafers (without socks), his voice is soft, breathless at times, like Marilyn Monroe's. His eyes are just as dark and riveting as they were at the Amblin meeting.

"I'm sorry it's so late," he apologizes. "I was rehearsing."

He pours himself some water and leans back in the armchair, taking a breath, and it's impossible not to stare at him endlessly. To watch the way he moves, so silky and gliding. He's taller than I expected. I'm 5' 7" and he must be at least 5'9" or 5'10." With a lean, strong body, but with the kind of shoulders you see on an adolescent boy: They haven't quite filled out yet.

"Where are you rehearsing?" I ask just to try out my voice. There's a shyness between us; I can feel it. I wonder if he has any idea how terrified I am. It's hard to conceive of him being frightened, someone so capable of standing in front of multitudes of people and performing. But in this setting, just one on one, he doesn't look comfortable. His nervousness seems to be mirroring mine. It's one thing for me, an agoraphobic, to be anxious, but I never expected to see it in Michael. I must admit I find it disarming.

I am charmed by this man.

I'm a professional, I remind myself. It's my job to get him to relax so we can work together. I somehow have to move past my own nerves to help him with his.

"You're recording an album?" I ask, my voice cracking until I clear it.

"We're recording in West Hollywood," he says, softly.

"I live in West Hollywood," I tell him. Not that he needs to know this, but I tell him anyway. Just to get the conversation flowing.

So far it's not.

"Where?" I ask him.

"Where?"

"Where in West Hollywood?"

"There's a recording studio on Santa Monica Blvd ..."

"I live one block up from Santa Monica."

"Where?" he asks.

"Where?"

"In West Hollywood?"

"Pointsettia"

Now *he's* staring at *me*.

"Are you kidding?" his voice raises higher, sounding very much like that "Ooh Hoo!" part in the *Beat It* video.

"No," I tell him. "I live there."

"That's where we rehearse!"

I'm stunned.

"The recording studio is right there on the corner! At Santa Monica and Poinsettia!" he says, in amazement.

"I know the building; it's at the end of our block!"

Maybe this is some sort of sign, I think, a good omen for the project. Whatever it is, it manages to break the ice for the two of us. Michael laughs, and I join him. All these years he's recorded just down the block from where I live. The coincidence of that somehow serves as a bridge to connect us, and we start to talk. We begin slowly, working our way around the formalities, talking about the lunch meeting we had with Steven. We exchange phone numbers, and he tells me I should come to his ranch.

"You have a ranch?" I ask him, thinking ponies and a barn filled with hay.

"Mm hm," he says. "It's beautiful! So relaxing."

I'm picturing a dude ranch in Montana, and wondering how the hell will I get there. I hope there's an Amtrak route because I hate to fly.

"I call it Neverland," he tells me. "It's just up the coast. It's beautiful! The most beautiful place in the world!"

He relaxes now as he starts to tell me about his Neverland, about how much he loves it, and how he delights in sharing it with underprivileged children.

"Kids that don't have anything, nothing at all. They come there, and they just have a ball! Some of them in wheelchairs, and on crutches; you should see the looks on their little faces, and how they laugh! They just forget all the bad things in their life. All the bad just goes away!"

"You're like Peter," I tell him.

He laughs, liking this.

"I'm just like Peter! My whole life I've been like Peter!"

Our shyness is slipping away now. The more we talk, the more comfortable I'm feeling. And I can see that Michael is becoming more relaxed too.

"That's why it's so important that we do this right. That this film be right!" he tells me. Urgently. Passionately.

"It has to be!" I assure him, "I love *Peter Pan!*"

"You do?" he giggles, surprised to find someone else willing to admit it.

"That's why I'm here. That's why I'm doing this!" I explain to him. "Ever since I was a kid, it's the one story that's meant the most to me. It helped me get through my childhood, and made me feel less lonely."

He's leaning forward now in the armchair, and I've forgotten my nerves as we talk about this story that captivated us in childhood and still holds our hearts as adults. We confess to the many times we've seen it and to the feelings it has always stirred. Discussing the power of J.M Barrie's storytelling, and the love we both have for his characters, we admit to one another just how much we both didn't want to grow up. For the first time all evening, I'm not looking at the borrowed watch on my wrist. The magic of Peter, the Lost Boys, Captain

Hook, and Neverland has captured us, connecting us as people, and making us forget the rest of the world.

The two hours pass quickly, and when I next peek at the time, it's almost 8 o'clock.

"I have to go!" I say to him urgently, like Cinderella at the ball at the stroke of midnight. I begin to pack up all of my notes and papers, replacing them back into my briefcase.

"Where are you going?" he asks, surprised at my sudden need to leave.

"It's almost 8. I have to go."

"You want to watch the Grammys with me?"

This stops me.

"The Grammys … ?"

Suddenly, I'm speechless. Stella told me to leave. She made a big point of it. "You must leave at 8. No excuses!"

I promised her I would leave. And my kids are sick, that's another reason I should leave. My kids are sick, and I'm their mommy. Sick kids need their mommy, and I should definitely go. I've already been here for two hours—that's more than enough time to be away from my house. My palms are starting to sweat. I really need to go. But how many times in my life will I be asked by Michael Jackson to watch the Grammys with him?

"This is fun! Please stay," Michael says, sensing my hesitation, and helping me to decide.

Well, maybe just the opening number.

The only television in the entire apartment is in Michael's bedroom.

Michael Jackson's bedroom.

Suddenly, I feel 14 again, and can't wait to run home and call all my girlfriends. "Ohmygodguesswhat! I was in his bedroom!" Am I star struck? Not usually. My three years as a tour guide with daily star sightings cured me of that. But I have to admit there's something magical and captivating about Michael. He's the biggest musical pop star in the world, and here I am alone with him in his bedroom.

I don't even have dreams like this.

Michael turns the set on and crawls on top of a large four-poster canopied bed. Okay, I don't know what the decorum is here. Do I crawl on top of the bed too? Too much too soon maybe? I look around for help; the bedroom is small and filled with books and papers, some of them stacked up on the floor. But there aren't a lot of chairs. Spying an empty one in the corner, I move over and take a seat. It's delicate, and it feels like an antique. I hope my sitting on it doesn't break it.

"You could sit up here," Michael tells me.

"I'm fine!" I smile, clutching my briefcase in my lap like some kind of security blanket.

My one chance to sit next to Michael Jackson on his own bed, and I had said no. To be honest, I was afraid I might faint.

And I doubted that would make me look very professional.

The Grammys start; live from the Los Angeles Shrine Auditorium, with Gary Shandling as the host. Michael's attention is riveted to the television screen.

"We're up for best video short," he says, excitedly. And I wonder why is he here in his bedroom, and not there, celebrating with the rest of the industry?

A phone rings on his nightstand, and Michael reaches for it. His voice is the most animated I've heard since meeting him, as he speaks excitedly, "Yes, I'm watching it right now. Are you watching it?"

I turn my attention to the Chevy commercial on the television set, and I try not to eavesdrop. Whoever Michael is speaking to is obviously someone he really cares about. I can hear the tender tone in his voice as he speaks gently, lovingly to the person at the other end of the line.

"Can we talk when it's over? Can I call you then?" he asks. "Okay!" he adds, signing off. "Love you!" He hangs up the phone, and turns to look over at me, "That's one of my kids!" he explains, excitedly.

"You have kids?" I ask him, not understanding. He wasn't married, and as far as I knew he didn't have any children.

"I have them all over the world, just like Peter," he explains. "They call me all the time, and we just talk about anything, anything at all. That's why I have this phone, so they can get in touch with me whenever they want. This is their own private number. They don't have to go through Stella or anyone else. If they need me, they know I'm always there for them, day or night. Just like Peter."

"Peter and the Lost Boys," I suggest, referring to the group of young boys that Peter Pan steals away from poor childhoods and bad parents, bringing them to live with him in Neverland.

"Mm hm," Michael says. "They're just like the Lost Boys in *Peter Pan*. And I'm Peter—I take care of them, and protect them."

Michael's face lights up as he talks about the boys. And I wonder: who are these kids in Michael's life?

The opening number of the Grammy's suddenly begins, and Michael turns his full attention to Billy Joel as he performs "We Didn't Start the Fire." All business now, he drums his hand along the side of his thigh, keeping time to the music.

"Good, that's good. No! Too soon! Got to hold longer on the entrance. Set up those drums—then enter." He talks directly to the television, feeling the music in his whole body and giving directions to an unreachable Billy Joel. "They needed more drums! Build the moment before the entrance, and then he can come in!" he says. "Don't you agree?" his eyes look over to mine for confirmation.

I nod. I smile. I'm amazed as I watch him working. He's like some magnificent thoroughbred racehorse locked in at the post, watching the other horses run. His muscles at the ready, his whole being is aching to be out there, wanting to be running with the rest. I watch him as he focuses on the music, studying Billy Joel's performance as the singer and the song become one. Michael looks the most relaxed I have seen since meeting him. Here with the music he looks comfortable. And safe. The way I feel when I'm sitting in my house.

"I have to go!" I say, suddenly remembering I'm not in my house. And realizing that fact is now giving me the chills.

"So soon?" Michael asks, seeming genuinely disappointed. "It just started!"

"My kids are sick," I explain, "I need to get back to them."

And back to my home.

But *that* I don't tell him.

He seems concerned, "What's wrong with your kids?"

Ear infections, I tell him, and he winces. We say our goodbyes, and I tell him I'll let myself out so he can keep watching the Grammys.

"We should tape these meetings," he says as I head for the door.

"Really?" I ask, never letting on that this meeting was tough enough, and the thought of going through another one is probably already raising my blood pressure.

"This project is very important to me."

I turn to look at him, and I can see in his eyes that he seems to mean it.

"Some day people will want to know about the making of this film," he explains, speaking in an almost reverent tone. "This is going to be film history!"

I can only hope.

I leave him for the night as the first awards are being handed out, and Michael is sitting at the end of his bed, watching intensely, all by himself. I'm thrilled that I've made it through the meeting, and I can finally go home now, but as I let myself out of the penthouse, I can't stop thinking of Michael. If he wins the Grammy, there won't be anyone with him to celebrate or to give him a hug. No one will be there to share his happiness, or to sit next to him, holding his hand in that long moment before his name is read. It seems ironic—the song he's nominated for is *Leave Me Alone.*

I can't help but wonder if he really means it.

6
Taking Flight with Peter
(If I Can Get Out of the House)

I had survived my first meeting with Michael.

Nothing bad had happened: I hadn't passed out or embarrassed myself by acting like a crazed fan or a generally neurotic screenwriter. I survived the drive there and back, and I was able to sit through a two and a half hour meeting without the room spinning or me breaking down in a total panic. More importantly, I hadn't received any frantic calls the next day from the studio, my agent, or Stella telling me that Michael hated me, and I was off the project. For most screenwriters, that's good news. But for me, the bad news was that I had to do this all over again in another two weeks when Michael would be free for another meeting.

I couldn't hide in the house anymore.

Michael Jackson was pulling me out of my front door and bringing me back into the world again. Whether I liked it or not.

At least I didn't have to worry that he'd ask me to go somewhere public where I didn't feel comfortable. Michael couldn't get out of his house either. Not because he didn't want to, but because he would've been mobbed. He had to dress up incognito, wearing masks or fake beards so he wouldn't be recognized. This meant we'd always be meeting at his Hideaway, and we'd never go out in public. No crowded restaurants or coffee houses. Or studio lots filled with people. We would just stay inside his Hideaway, the two of us, and never go out.

Michael was an agoraphobic's perfect writing partner.

Project M was different than any other film project I had ever worked on. I had never developed a script for a star before. Usually, I was hired on as the screenwriter, but I never knew who would be playing the lead role. But this time I knew who would be saying the lines I'd be writing. I'd be able to hear Michael's voice in my head, the cadence of his speech, and watch his movements in my imagination as I developed scenes. This is helpful for a screenwriter.

But it comes with a price.

I wasn't kidding myself: Project M was 90% about the writing, and 100% about keeping Michael happy. Being able to get along with him, listening to his ideas, and making him feel comfortable was just as important as those words I'd be putting on the page. I wasn't just writing *Peter Pan*; I was writing Michael's *Peter Pan* and holding his hand while I did it. I only hoped I was up to the task.

The writing didn't concern me.

The other part did.

While I waited for a phone call from Stella letting me know when Michael would be ready to meet with me again, I started to do my research and think out an outline.

This was easier said than done in a house with two small kids. Being an agoraphobic meant that I had always written at home. It wasn't difficult when Jacob and Kathryn were infants, but now they were walking, talking, and demanding, "Where's Mommy?" No matter how many times you tell a child, "Mommy is working. She needs alone time in her office," you are using words that are out of the decibel range for their tiny (but cute) ears. They know where Mommy is, and once they know they will hunt you down relentlessly hour after hour after hour.

I tried everything in my power to keep myself in, and my children out of my small home office. Locks. Bolts. Barricading the door with furniture. Or simply pretending I wasn't in there. I would ask them to knock, and they'd say, "Okay, Mommy" in their sweetest of voices. And then they'd run back into my office in ten minutes to ask, "Are you still working?" It didn't take me long to figure out that writing at home wasn't going to be an option for Project M. I had to find somewhere else to write.

The problem was how to get there.

"I need an office." I announce to my husband one night

as we were slipping into bed. "In a child-free zone." I suggest. "Somewhere I don't have to break up fights, fix broken toys, and kiss boo-boos."

"Just lock the door."

Spoken like a true father.

"That doesn't work, David." I explain. "Jacob keeps pounding, and Kathryn just screams." I wait for a sympathetic sound from his side of the bed. Not getting it, I nudge him to make sure he's not asleep. "I need an office outside of the house," I announce, bravely.

David stares at me like I'm speaking Dutch, a language in fact, that neither one of us knows.

"You'd have to leave the house every day to get there," my loving husband points out to me.

Good point. And usually a deal breaker. But this was a complicated project I was being asked to write, a story demanding all of my attention. I couldn't be worrying that while I was flying in a scene over Neverland Kathryn might burst in demanding a potty break.

"I'll never be able to find Neverland if I don't leave the house," I say.

David smiles. To most people, this might sound a little bit crazy. But when your husband is an actor, it makes perfect sense to him.

"How are you going to do this?" he asks me, gently.

"Maybe if I don't go too far?" I suggest, testing the water. "I don't have to go all the way across town to get an office."

I'd been thinking about this ever since that first phone call from Disney. My days of working at home seemed numbered. It would only be a matter of time before I'd have to take that first big step out into the world to find a quiet, secure place to work. It hadn't much mattered between writing assignments or on jobs that were less demanding. I could find a way to work around the kids, writing at night or when they took naps or were in school. But Project M was more demanding. Meeting with Michael at odd times and for who knows how long would mean I'd have to be ready, focused, and at the top of my game. I needed to create my own Neverland: a place I could go anytime I wanted.

I needed a real office.

One day as I watched David wheeling Jacob and Kathryn in their red wagon down the sidewalk, I thought I'd found my answer.

At the end of our street, directly across a large and busy boulevard, was a studio lot that took up an entire city block. Originally built by Charlie Chaplin, Mary Pickford, and Douglas Fairbanks Jr., it was called United Artists in the 1920s when the three stars formed their own company. Charlie Chaplin even built an apartment house at the other end of our street where he stayed when he was working. I once made friends with someone living in that Chaplin building just so I could tour the small-scale apartment with miniature doorways and stairs built especially for Chaplin's short stature. A man who loved being within eyeshot of his home was a man I dearly admired.

"Do you know that studio at the end of the block?" I ask David, who has probably auditioned at every studio in town.

"Warner Brothers owns it. I've had meetings there," he confirms.

"In an office?"

"Yes, an office," he laughs.

"Without children?!" I ask, hopefully.

"Not a kid in sight," he says, kissing me goodnight.

It sounded promising.

Getting my office was the easy part.

Warner Brothers Hollywood had small spaces to rent. They didn't care if I was working for Disney (their competitor), as long as I could pay the rent each month; that's what counted. But getting to the office would be much more difficult.

It was only a block away but impossible to reach.

Walking to the studio was out of the question: I had a fear of open spaces (especially when they're filled with people) so being on a sidewalk (even for a block) was not about to happen. I could always have someone drop me off and pick me up, and I tried this for a few days during the first week. But it just didn't feel right being on the lot. There were too many people and too many cars. It was noisy, and I couldn't relax when I was there; I didn't feel comfortable at all. I just kept thinking,

"When the hell can I go home?" You can't write a lot of movie scenes when all you're thinking about is punching out your timecard. Somehow I needed to make my office a safe and comfortable space. It had to become like my second home.

That's when I decided to try the unthinkable.

"I need the car," I announce to David as I collapse on the couch after an hour-long Dr. Seuss reading marathon to get the kids to sleep.

"You need the car, and why?" he asks, certain that he must have misheard me.

"Driving the car to the studio will mean that my car will be in the parking lot."

He looks over and waits for me to continue.

I thought I was making sense, but clearly, he needed more information.

"And who's going to drive the car there?" he asks, more confused than ever.

"Me?" I say, reaching for his glass of wine and sipping it for confidence.

"*You're* going to drive it," he repeats, just to make sure he understands.

I try to explain, the words stumbling out of me.

"I need to feel safe at the office…and comfortable. But there's nothing that's familiar to me there. I don't know the people. I don't know the buildings. There are so many buildings, David!" I tell him, starting to feel the nerves kick in.

"There are a lot of buildings," he says in agreement, taking his wine back. "No way you can get around that, the buildings or the people."

"I know! It's scary!"

"So why do you need the car?"

"When I went to my first meeting with Michael, it helped knowing I had a car waiting for me. Knowing that if I had a problem—like a sudden earthquake, or if I panicked, or the kids needed me—I could just go outside, and the car would be there. Just sitting there. Waiting to take me home."

David nods: he's actually following my logic.

"But you had a driver," he suggests.

Most of my logic.

"And the driver is the one who drove you home," he explains, as though I'm suffering from some momentary memory lapse. "You're afraid to drive, remember?"

"Okay, that's the part I haven't worked out yet," I admit.

He smiles.

"That's a big part."

"Unless I'm the driver," I say hesitantly.

I can't believe I'm suggesting this.

"I mean…It would be a big, big, really big step for me," I say. "…but this whole project is a big step."

David agrees with a silent, yet sensitive nod.

"I like our car—it reminds me of you and the kids," I explain. "So if it's at the studio, I can look out my window, and maybe I won't see all those buildings and all the people. I won't think about Michael or Steven or all the stress and the pressure. I'll just see our Taurus, and it'll remind me that I'm not that far from home—that a little bit of home is right there. Sitting in the parking lot."

He looks at me to see if I'm kidding.

I'm not.

"I need to drive to the studio every day so I can work."

"Can you do that?" he asks, amazed at what I'm suggesting.

I was pretty sure that I couldn't.

But if I wanted to write *Peter Pan* for Michael I knew I better try.

Every great expedition begins with a first step. Mine was just getting into the car. I tried it the next day, sitting in the front seat, the first time behind a steering wheel in years. I waited for the nerves to hit me, and they did. But I made myself a promise from the moment I climbed into our Ford that I would take things slowly. If all I did was sit in the front seat all morning, it would be some kind of progress.

At least I hoped.

I didn't go very far those first few days. As a matter of fact, I didn't go anywhere at all. But I got used to being in the driver's seat again without feeling panicky. That took a couple of days. After that, I found the courage to adjust the seat and buckle myself in. It was only a block to the studio. Well, a couple of blocks because there was no traffic signal at the end of our street. I'd have to drive around the block and down to the corner. More than a couple of blocks, two and a half blocks really. A small distance for anyone else but for me, an impossibility. Less than three blocks separated me from the studio and an office where I could build Neverland, populating it with Peter, the Lost Boys, Tinkerbell, and Captain Hook.

I just had to find a way to turn on the ignition.

7
The Hideaway

My next meeting with Michael would be at the Hideaway again.

It was going to be a late one—after 9 p.m., and Stella apologized for the time. She knew I had little children, but I assured her not to worry, they'd be in bed and asleep by the time I left.

Wishful thinking.

Jacob and Kathryn knew I was going out to meet with Michael so no one was interested in sleeping, and no amount of pleading (or reading stories) could keep them in their beds. They were half dressed in jammies, covered in chocolate ice cream (a last minute bribe), not bathed (I tried but got soaked), and far from ready for "night-night." By the time the car arrived to pick me up, David had his arms filled with two crying kids who didn't understand (or care) why Mommy was going out at bedtime.

It wasn't easy leaving them, but having a Town Car and driver waiting in the driveway with the motor running helped. I jumped in the backseat and made a fast getaway to the sounds of kids wailing in the night.

I was exhausted, and the meeting with Michael hadn't even started yet.

Tonight we're watching *Peter Pan*.

Michael owns a copy of the Hallmark 25th Anniversary Special starring Mia Farrow and Danny Kaye, and he has the VHS tape of the 1977 production waiting for me when I arrive.

Once again it's just the two of us, and I'm still surprised that there aren't any personal assistants or housekeepers around. This really is a hideout for Michael. He's on his own here, and that amazes me. For someone used to being taken care of or pampered, he almost seems happy to be here by himself.

"I'm sorry we have to watch this on such a small screen," he says, as he slips the videocassette out of its sleeve.

A television set has somehow mysteriously appeared in the living room, along with a VHS player. Michael slides the tape into the machine and hesitates as he tries to figure out which buttons to push.

Do I help him? Do I not?

I let him take a moment to figure it out, just as I would with one of my kids. When he really gets too stuck, I offer some assistance. Together we figure it out and set up the tape to play.

"We'll watch the Disney cartoon at Neverland," Michael promises me. "On the big screen!" he says excitedly, his eyes widening at the thought of it.

I'm trying *not* to think of it.

Neverland Ranch is hours away, and it sounds so big and overwhelming. It's hard enough just going across town to the Hideaway. But going to Neverland is a major road trip. It'll take hours to get there, and hours to come back home again. I tell myself not to worry about it: one meeting at a time becomes my new mantra.

"Do you want a soft drink?" Michael asks me with a smile. "I've got snacks!" he tells me, seeming proud to actually be entertaining here in his own place.

I go into the kitchen to grab a 7-Up from the fridge, and I notice bags of chips sitting on the counter. When I go back into the living room I catch Michael happily setting out bowls of pistachio nuts in their shells and cheese and chives potato chips on an end table near my easy chair.

I feel like I'm on a middle school date.

When he is sure I have the most comfortable of seats, and all of my needs are attended to ("Do you want anything else, Darlene?"), he finally clicks off the lights and presses the play button on the video machine. Suddenly, we are transported to the first of many Neverlands we will visit together.

In the dark, I try to concentrate on the images on the

screen, but I find my attention sneaking over to look at Michael as he watches the story unfold. Laughing at all of the funny bits and intensely quiet during the serious moments, he's like a little kid knowing what comes next and delighting in the certainty of it. I'm sure he must have watched this tape dozens of times, but his attention is as focused as if this is his first viewing. Only when he says a line of dialogue along with one of the actors on the screen does it reveal just how intimately Michael knows this story. The video is so worn from him watching it that the tape breaks three quarters of the way through.

Michael is disappointed that we can't finish the film and wants to track down another copy for me to view at his Neverland Ranch.

"No, that's all right," I assure him, once again silently saying my mantra so the thought of Neverland doesn't totally freak me out.

"You have to see Disney's *Peter Pan* on a big screen," he insists. "We can watch it at Neverland."

One meeting a time. One meeting at a time...

"Will the studio send you a copy?" I ask.

"I own a copy," he says, matter-of-factly, "35mm with full Dolby Sound."

I'm impressed.

"Do you think we can wait a few weeks before we see it?' he asks. "Will that be all right?"

"I think it can wait," I assure him, relieved to be staying in town.

At least for the moment.

In the meantime, I suggest to him that we take a look at the original text that J.M. Barrie wrote. This was my cue to reach into my briefcase and pull out a special surprise. I had spent a week tracking down and buying a copy of Barrie's 1911 novel, *Peter and Wendy*, to give to Michael as a gift. I wanted something to commemorate the beginnings of this project and our collaboration together. I located an original copy of the novel at a rare bookstore in Beverly Hills, and I pull out the book to show it to him.

"I bought you a gift," I say.

He suddenly looks overwhelmed with shyness.

"You did?"

I hold out the old edition of *Peter and Wendy*.

His eyes light up as he takes the gift from me.

"Oh!" he says, softly, in appreciation. "This is a wonderful book!" Eagerly, he flips through the pages, searching for the pictures.

I get the feeling he's seen this book before.

"I love the illustrations in this version!"

As a matter of fact, I think he might already own it.

"Um...do you have this version?" I ask, hoping that he doesn't.

"Mm hm," he says, in all innocence.

Of course, I never thought of this when I bought it. How do you possibly give a gift to someone who already has everything?

The fact that Michael already owns the book doesn't seem to matter to him; he thanks me for it, and I'm touched by his sincerity. He makes a point of showing me some of the illustrations, and his kindness makes me feel comfortable and welcomed.

Reaching into my workbag again, I pull out my small tape recorder.

Michael watches as I set it up on the table between us.

"Is this okay?" I ask him, double-checking to make sure he hasn't changed his mind about recording these meetings.

"Oh yes!" he says.

Already loaded with a 90-minute cassette, the machine sits at the ready as I press the red button marked "Record."

And slowly, we begin to work.

8
Off the Record

Collaborating on a film script involves two people sitting in a room separated by the silence of two minds working together. When you collaborate with another person, you spend stretches of time without speaking. The more you know someone, the more comfortable you get with each other's pauses. Sometimes what isn't said can be more important than what is actually spoken.

Michael isn't talking, and I don't know what that means.

As soon as I clicked on the tape recorder, he stopped speaking. The conversation had been so easy between us, but now there's only silence. I'm not sure whether he wants me to lead the discussion, if he's just being polite or if he expects me to come up with all of the ideas. I wait for him to say something, to give me a clue, and when he doesn't, I decide I better jump in.

"I jotted down some notes when I read the novel of *Peter and Wendy*," I tell him. "That's how I start an adaptation—looking for clues in the source material."

"Mm hmm," he says, waiting for more.

I pick up the book and search for something, anything to get this ball rolling.

"Okay, here, for example is Barrie's interpretation of children," I say, and begin to read from the book.

"Mm hmm."

Michael says "Mm hmm" a lot. It seems to be his way of letting me know he's listening. It's polite; I like it. The way he stretches out the syllables, lingering for a moment on one or the other lets me know how he's feeling.

"There's a sweetness to children on one hand…"

"Hmmmm." He says and smiles, knowingly.

"And on the other hand… a sneakiness."

"Hmmm" he says, and giggles.

The room grows quiet, and I want to ask him what prompted the giggle. Instead, I let the silence linger for a moment, and it grows until I realize that if I don't keep this conversation going, it's not going to go anywhere.

"You know what I felt reading the book? It was the first time I really got a hit on the Lost Boys. I saw five definite personalities."

"Hmmmmmmm," he says with conviction.

I seem to be on to something here. So I keep going.

"I think it's important that we see each boy as a definite character."

"Yeah."

It's the first word Michael has spoken since I've turned on

the tape recorder. I've managed to unlock the silence, and he's now finally beginning to speak.

"The whole thing with the Lost Boys gotta make sense," he says with great conviction, sounding more "street" than I've ever heard him before. Suddenly, he's lively, and animated. "Where do they come from? Is it real to you how they got there? To Neverland? Or is it just fairy tale stuff?"

"They're orphans; they have no family."

"But how'd they get to Neverland?"

"Peter picked them up. He found them," I explain.

I'm not sure if Michael is testing me to see how much I know about *Peter Pan*, or if he's just like Jacob and Kathryn who ask me questions when they don't understand something in a story.

"That's nice." Michael smiles. "And Peter brought them to Neverland because they didn't have anyone?" he asks, making sure of this point.

I tell him yes, and he smiles again.

"That's good!" he says, showing his excitement.

I feel like I've passed a pop quiz.

We now have our first character point, and we build on it.

"You see, Peter does this," I suggest. "That's what he's done with Wendy, Michael, and John. He's been watching their family—and he's seen parents who are at work a lot. In the play and in the novel, the mother was a wonderful mother," I explain. "She was there all the time for her children."

"Mm hmm."

I start to think of my own children, and I wonder if they're asleep now or calling out for me and wanting me to be back home. I can't help feeling a little bit guilty for not being there. Is this why I don't like to leave the house?

"Life's different now than when *Peter Pan* was first written. Everybody's on this treadmill. Fathers work. Mothers work. Kids don't spend very much time with their parents."

I'm saying this to myself as much as I am to Michael.

"There's a good movie you gotta see!" Michael says, excitedly. "It was on 'The Twilight Zone.' It has so much heart! And it reminds me of Peter. Called *Kick the Can*. Gotta see it! Next time we meet, I'm showing you!" He laughs at the thought of it, brimming over with enthusiasm. "It has heart about it! *That* should be Peter!"

"What's it about?"

"It's about this old man who stays in this convalescent home, and someone told him that his son had called him— he was coming to pick him up, to take him out for the evening to have dinner or something. So the old man packs his bags, suitcases, and everything. His son picks him up, and he sees his father with these suitcases like he's coming to stay with him. His son tells him he misunderstood, 'I just came to say hi to you, that's all.' So he says goodbye to his father; they have an argument and..." He pauses purposefully to build the dramatic moment, and then, grins. "I don't want to give it away."

I laugh. He's played me.

"You're gonna like it!" He beams. "It's got heart!" he shouts. "You gotta see it!" He lowers his voice and says slowly, "It's wonderful!" Snapping his fingers for effect, "It has in it what Peter should have! Oh and it's beautiful in the end!"

"Well, don't tell me," I warn him with a laugh. And he laughs too.

"Yeah, I won't."

"*Kick the Can*?"

"Mm hm … Mm Hmmmmm!" he says with emphasis.

The room grows silent again. Suddenly, I hear a little giggle. I look over at Michael—he is smiling broadly, staring at me like a kid with a big secret.

"What?" I ask him, but he just keeps grinning at me. "What?!"

He whispers, "You got to see *Kick the Can*!"

I laugh because he reminds me of my five-year-old son who never lets go of an idea until he gets what he wants.

"It's great! When I saw it, I loved it! And I thought, 'This is me! This is *me*! *This* is *me*!'"

"Really?"

"Yeah, I loved it!" He's laughing now, and let's loose with one of his famous high-pitched "Hoo, hoo, hoo!"

"Well, next time we meet we'll see it." I assure him in my motherhood tone of voice I always use with my kids. To keep them on track and to get them to do what I want. "You know when you just laughed right now," I tell him, with a leap of faith, and a hope that I'm not getting too personal. "You know the quality you have that's just perfect for Peter?" I pause for effect, and he leans in a little. "There's a mischievous side of you."

Michael giggles like a boy with his hand caught stealing freshly baked cookies.

"Oh yeah!" He agrees and chuckles some more.

"That's a part of Peter," I tell him. "And that's an important quality because there's a fun-loving side to him. Peter loves life! And that has to be in our film."

"You're right. You're absolutely right. To do what he's doing to Hook, playing with him the way he does," he says.

"That really makes Hook angry," I suggest. "He does not like to be played with."

"Especially by a boy," he interjects. "Hook's got to be terrible. Where you hate him!"

Captain Hook is Peter Pan's nemesis in the story. When the play first opened in 1902, Hook was such a villain that he caused little children to cry and to hold onto their parents in terror. Over the years, Hook's character has evolved into a foppish, gentlemanly semi-comic bad guy. But in the novel Hook is described as a villain to be feared.

I reach for a handful of pistachios left over from our screening. I notice that Michael hasn't eaten any of the snacks he laid out on the table. It's the second time I've been with him when food has been around, and I've noticed he hasn't eaten anything. I sip on my 7-up, but Michael is only drinking water. The mother in me worries.

Michael tells me adamantly that he doesn't want to soften the Captain Hook character for the film. Traditionally, the same actor who plays the father of the three children Peter befriends also plays Captain Hook. At the Amblin lunch, Steven had suggested doing the same for our film. Michael was strangely quiet at the idea. In our first private meeting he had suggested that casting only one actor might break a certain reality needed in the portrayal of such a villainous character.

"Do you think Steven will be open to not having the father be the same actor as Captain Hook?" I ask.

"We can convince him of that," Michael says without hesitation.

We? As in Michael Jackson and me against Steven Spielberg?! This is tricky. Align myself with Michael, and I risk alienating Steven who could replace me. But if Michael senses I'm not falling in line with him, *he* can replace me. Smart screenwriter that I am, I know how to play this: look pensive and just listen.

"We can show him how we feel that it's only right for Captain Hook to be Captain Hook. Real, cold-hearted, and another person, not the father. Someone who's threatening Neverland and Peter."

I nod thoughtfully without committing one way or the other.

"Hook is trying to take over the whole place—like people do with countries," he explains. "He's a greedy old pig! I love the thing Steven said where Hook is destroying Neverland, where we see how the place transforms."

This is something Michael and Steven both agree on: safe territory for me to explore.

"Like someone taking over paradise to build condominiums," I suggest.

"That's exactly what it is!" he says, liking the comparison.

Score one for the screenwriter.

"Cutting down all the forests," I say, confidently.

"Like the way the world is being affected today." He thinks for a moment, "When they first get to Neverland it should be this most beautiful, magical, gorgeous place ever seen… Paradise! Then there's the other side we show that is being threatened: the land is changing; it's just so ugly. And Peter explains to Wendy, Michael, and John that pretty soon all of Neverland is going to be like this if we don't…"

He stops and searches for something to complete the thought.

I wait him out.

"…Whatever, whatever… something like that."

Sometimes you fill in the blanks, and other times knowing a blank is there waiting to be filled is at least a good start. Michael doesn't seem to be afraid of suggesting something even if he doesn't have the finish. I wish I could be that brave. I'm always afraid I might say something stupid and be asked to leave the party.

"Neverland is being destroyed," he says. "We show some of this other side… there would be another section of Neverland that's just terrible… ugly, polluted. And these pirates who are pigs have done this. And all Hook cares about is greed and money. He's destroying the place. Fish are dying, and the mermaids. It should be a serious threat to the land and the kids. This place was once a beautiful paradise. And then … at the end when Hook is killed, we see this other thing happen. It would be so uplifting, don't you think? And rewarding. We see all those fairies go up, and the land changes again, and the heavens open up. Neverland is back to what it should be. And the kids are jumping up and down."

"You see the transformation," I confirm.

"The fish are swimming again, and the rainbow is complete."

"I think Captain Hook is such an evil presence that even the animals sense it, and have left." I suggest.

Michael laughs; he likes this.

"There are no animals living on that one section of the island," I say.

"They've been killing and shooting the animals," he adds. "Just like planet earth."

We're working together now, starting to see moments and characters.

"For dinner we could see Captain Hook having a feast with his guys, but seeing them prepare it, torturing these animals," Michael says, the words pouring out of him. "Something where, you know, you see these things tied up. Instead of just doing it to eat, they're having fun with torturing the animals to kill them. We have to really hate these guys, I think."

"It's important," I say.

"Very important," Michael agrees with a nod of his head. "I hope Steven doesn't disagree," he says abruptly. "We can *not* have Captain Hook singing. As soon as he opens his mouth to sing, it's all watered down. It's being light-hearted. Like what if the witch in *The Wizard of Oz* was singing, and her and the flying monkeys were dancing?"

"That's a good example!" I say. "If Steven has problems with this idea then definitely we should bring up the witch."

Michael reaches out to the *Peter and Wendy* novel on the footstool that sits between his armchair and mine. He thumbs through the book, looking at the pictures.

"Does the whole thing about Peter not knowing what a kiss is, and giving Wendy an acorn instead of a kiss work for you?" I ask.

"It's stupid," he says softly, lost in the book. "Doesn't make sense."

"And what about when they fly into Neverland, and Wendy is shot by an arrow, but then she's miraculously okay." I ask him.

"That is so stupid."

"Stupid, I agree." I parrot back to him.

"You can't have any of those weak moments like that. Got to be strong connections, strong foundations. *Peter Pan* is about digging for that child inside of everyone, and playing with its emotions." He sets down the book, and looks over at me curiously, "How old is Peter? I mean he could be a thousand years old! Should that be brought up or something? He's been doing this for generations upon generations, and ages and ages," Michael tells me.

"He could be as old as all time," I suggest.

He locks eyes with me and speaks imploringly, "But when Peter comes, whatever you do, Darlene…it should be so magical. That you love his world, you love his presence and his aura. There should be something magical about Peter…you can feel it! And Tink just enhances the magic. The fact that she's with him…this magical thing from another world."

"I don't know if you should actually see Tinkerbell—you see the light of Tinkerbell," I suggest. "But I don't think you should reveal her features right away."

"With the special effects today, you can really do that," Michael says, excitedly. "We could plan it where she flies across Peter's face, and a beautiful blue lights up his face. Very magical! Or when he holds her in his hand, the reflection on his face as he's talking to her, you can see it in his eyes. It is so beautiful! You go 'Wow!' Then she changes colors according to how she feels."

"Oh, that's good!" I say, encouraging him. The more ideas Michael comes up with, the less work I have to do as a screenwriter. "That would be great!" I gush, hoping he'll continue filling out a scene, a moment, a character trait.

My motives here aren't exactly noble.

Silence fills the room again as we both try to picture the unborn scene in our minds. Michael closes his eyes to see the images beginning to form.

"So pretty!" he whispers. "On fire! That scene's got to be brilliant, the special effects, the flying scene. Just incredible. You have to want to be there!"

His enthusiasm is contagious. I'm beginning to feel like I'm a little girl again: fearless and in love with adventure.

"It would be wonderful if we could see them flying with birds," I suggest.

Michael smiles, still with his eyes closed.

"Can you imagine if a bird is flying…" I say.

"Yeah!" he says, seeing it in his mind.

"The bird would practically do a double take…"

"I know!!!!"

"…Looking at all these people flying along next to him."

"You can do that, that's possible!"

If Michael says it's possible, then I know it's possible.

"Are we going to do the scene where Tink is dying?" he asks quietly.

"I think we have to."

"We should really believe she's dead though. We should see her light go out."

"I want to milk that moment as much as we can," I tell him.

"Milk it!" he agrees loudly. "When you see her light just slowly dim…and with that dimming, the emotions of the kids—they should be bawling. And Peter should be pleading with her, 'Don't die! We've done everything together!'"

Michael is acting it out, slipping easily into Peter.

Suddenly, he drops character.

"Does she die? Does she come back at the end? We could root her back or something," he suggests.

He's up on his feet now and feeling the emotions of the scene.

"I think if she dies Peter should be on fire! I mean steaming angry! And now the big showdown is on!" Acting it out, "'You killed Tink, my buddy for thousands of years!'"

Michael is putting on a show, and I'm the only one in the audience. I'm delighted and captivated.

"We got to just get people wired up, get them cooking!" he says. "Then when she comes back, there's applause, and there's screaming. And all of the fairies are coming back. It's like jubilation!!!"

"That's great!" I tell him, resisting the urge to applaud.

"Where did Peter come from?" he suddenly asks.

"Barrie wrote that as a baby Peter took flight out of the nursery, through the window," I explain. "Then when he came back one day, his mother had put bars on the window, and there was another baby in the crib. And that's when he realized she didn't want him anymore."

The sadness of that passage hits me, reminding me of my own children. I'm starting to feel too comfortable here with Michael, getting lost in our imaginations and in Barrie's world. I suddenly want to be home with my kids. But we're making progress together, and I can't stop until I sense Michael wants to stop. It's 90% writing, I remind myself. And 100% keeping Michael happy.

"Our biggest mistake is to play down to kids in any of this. To make it cutesy. It be serious stuff: real serious-serious," he says, showing no signs of wanting this meeting to be over. "If we make Peter Pan twinkle toes, we're in trouble. Right now he's known as a guy who wears tights, and flies, and helps those little kids. He's got to be a guy that's adventurous, and he's tough. He has heart, but he can be bad too."

I wonder what he means by this? What's Peter's bad side?

"Steven wants some kind of connection with Hook and the kids," he tells me. "Having the same actor play the father. But it can't be that. To me we should have surprises," he says strongly.

His tone of voice has changed; he seems stronger. The boyishness and sense of fun has disappeared. This is a side of Michael I haven't seen before.

Abruptly, he reaches over and shuts off the tape recorder. Mumbling softly, he says, "I don't know who's going to hear these tapes."

I assume we might be done for the night. But not yet.

"I'm worried about Steven," he confides to me, softly. With the tape no longer recording, he's free to say what he wants. "Do you think he can do this?"

"Do this?"

I'm lost and not following.

"Do this film?" I ask him, trying to understand what he means.

"Do you think he has the heart to make *Peter Pan*?"

I'm shocked by the question: Michael Jackson is asking me what I think of Steven Spielberg's directing capabilities. I'm the only one in the room who is a Hollywood nobody. The visitor in Neverland, I'm just Wendy in this tale, the one who doesn't really belong here.

I quickly do a silent inventory in my mind of the recent Spielberg films: *Empire of the Sun, Always, The Color Purple.* They're not exactly in the same blockbuster category of *Jaws, Close Encounters,* and *E.T.* Did they have heart, or is Michael really saying they weren't film classics? He wants to make his *Peter Pan* a film classic; he's just not sure that Steven is the director who can help him do that.

"I've had other directors come to me about *Peter Pan,* but I always wanted to do this with Steven," Michael says. He seems genuine about his respect for the man, but his apprehension about the director seems real too. "But I don't know...I don't know if he can handle the heart of the story. I saw what he did in *Twilight Zone,* the way he adapted *Kick the Can.* That's in the *Twilight Zone* movie he did. He took *Kick the Can,* and put it in the movie, and it's not as good as the original. You'll see what I mean. I want you to see both, and Steven's isn't as good. The heart isn't there. I'm not sure he has heart like he used to."

How do I play this? Do I defend Steven? Do I tell Michael I have the same doubts even if I don't? How much do I have to lie just to keep him happy?

"I think he can do this," I assure him. "We just have to guide him along the way, and make sure he makes the *Peter Pan* you want to make. If we work together, knowing what we want on the page, we can make sure that Steven does the film the way we think the story should be told."

Michael nods, thinking about it, letting the possibilities of the project, and the ideas for the story mingle together for a moment.

I hold my breath, hoping I haven't lost him.

Reaching his hand out, Michael turns on the tape recorder again, and presses "Record." Sitting back now in his chair, he breaks out in a big smile.

"How good I would feel for what we've done right! Controlling the audience, taking them where we want in these scenes. And to hear them sniffling, and hear them laughing, to hear them…clapping, applauding!" He absolutely explodes with excitement, "It's so good inside! Really! After all the hard work." He moans a little, "Ohhhhhhh! We'd have them in the palm of our hands! We can do it! And we will do it!"

He has so much confidence I can't help but believe it's possible.

"This is very, very, very good, and very special to me," he says. "I love the idea of *Peter Pan*, I love it! And it's really never been done right. It's a perfect vehicle to touch the world. Cause it's that transition everybody has to deal with—about growing up. Everybody can relate to it. People say, 'I remember when I felt like that.' I still feel that way! Nobody wants to admit that they really don't want to grow up. They want to fit into society and play it cool. But inside they're just…kids."

He looks directly into my eyes.

"We're going to make an incredible movie," he says, softly. "I feel it. I know it!"

His enthusiasm is catching.

"Everything we've talked about I can see through Spielberg's camera," I say excitedly. "The way Steven shoots and the look of his…"

Before I can finish my thought, Michael has reached over to shut off the recorder again. The tape stops in place, and there is silence. Michael fills it when he finally says, "We have to make him see things our way."

The words are cold and unemotional, sounding more like a threat than a conspiracy.

"We will," I assure him.

And I know now that our meeting for the night is over.

9
Getting to the Office
(Wishful Thinking)

Writers will find any excuse not to write.

A phone ringing. Spots on a carpet. Furniture that needs to be re-arranged. I have never done more laundry in my life than at times when I've been avoiding sitting down and writing.

My contract had been signed; I was already meeting with Michael; I had books that had to be read, and ideas Michael and I had discussed that I needed to flesh out. The kids were at school (at least for a few hours); I had the house to myself (until they came home); my computer hummed at the ready (with no kids barging into my office). So why was I busy scraping Play Doh off the playroom floor?

This is why mommy writers need offices away from the house.

But I had an office now that was just a few blocks away. The solitude that I needed was just sitting there waiting for me. All I had to do was go into that office, shut the door, and leave the world, with all of its distractions, behind me.

If I could just get to my office.

After a week of practicing my driving (i.e. sitting behind the wheel with the engine off) I was still stuck in neutral. No matter how many times I attempted it, I just couldn't pull the damn car out of the driveway. Every time I tried, I'd give up, retreating back into the house and ordering Chinese food for the night. It took everything in my power not to just climb into bed and pull the blankets over my head in exasperation. But Mommy hiding under the bed covers eating Mu Shu pork was not a childhood memory I wanted to hand down to my kids.

Feeling sorry for myself wasn't going to get me out of the house. I just had to keep trying every day and not give up. More importantly, I didn't want to stress out about it. This project was stressful enough. Just sitting in a room alone with Michael Jackson made my pulse race. I didn't need anything else to worry about.

That's when the phone rang.

How could I not answer it? I was a writer trying to write.

"So?" Howard asks at the other end of the line.

"So?" I repeat, not having a clue.

"How's it going?!"

I took a wild guess.

"With Michael?"

"Don't make me beg," Howard warns me.

"It's great!!! He's wonderful! It's so exciting! I sat in his bedroom and watched the Grammys with him!" I gush.

"How's the work coming?" I could almost hear him snapping his studio whip. "That's why we're paying you, you know. Not to sit there and drool."

"He's very shy. It's going to take time to get him to trust me, and open up."

"You're not his therapist. You're a screenwriter." Howard reminds me.

"I want him to feel comfortable, Howard. It's part of my process." That last line was something an older, wiser screenwriter once mentored me to use when studio suits and producers needed definite answers in story meetings. "Never tell them anything," the old sage had advised. "Just say it's part of your process."

"How long are the meetings?" Howard asks, and I could envision him filling out a timecard at the other end.

"The first one was only two hours, but the last meeting went much longer. Do I get overtime, Howard?"

"Did you really watch the Grammys with him?" he asks, and for the first time I detect just the slightest tone of envy.

"In his bedroom," I say, emphasizing each word dramatically. "He sat on top of his bed, Howard. Would you like to know what he was wearing?"

Was that a slight intake of breath at the other end of the phone? Could this steely hearted, strictly business-minded, cool-as-ice executive possibly be a fan?

"I'm wondering if maybe I should come to these meetings," he suggests.

Yep, a fan.

"Howard, you have to trust that I can do this without you there to make it happen. I know what you want; I know how to do it; I can get the job done. Michael's excited about having these story meetings. I've coaxed Bambi out of the woods, and I will deliver him to you, all wrapped up in a pretty bow, along with a great script."

If I can only get to my office to write it.

This of course I don't tell him.

"He's not coming up with strange ideas, is he?"

I decide not to mention Michael's concern about Steven. It was off the record. My lips were sealed.

"Of course not!"

"If they're strange, just ignore them."

"I can handle this, Howard."

"But if I'm there with you I can keep him on track…"

"Howard, this is part of my process. Don't question it!"

With that said, Howard did what every other executive does when a screenwriter starts talking about process. He got bored and hung up.

It wasn't long before Raymond called.

"Is he strange?"

"Who?" I ask, seriously wondering if he meant Howard.

"Wacko Jacko. What did his skin look like? I hear he uses bleach. He has a skin condition, you know? Impetigo or something. It causes blotches."

I stick the phone in the crook of my neck as I bend down

to pick up an assortment of cast away dolls, stuffed animals, toy trucks, and a half-eaten pop tart.

"He looks fine, Raymond. No blotches. No abnormalities. He seems like a perfectly decent human being. Very polite. Well mannered. He actually served me potato chips and pistachios all by himself!"

"Howard's right. You have a crush."

"Howard wants to crash our meetings. *He* has the crush."

"When are you seeing him again?" he asks, sounding like my best high school girlfriend asking how things were going with the football jock.

"I'm waiting for a call."

"Does he call you?!" he asks with bated breath.

"His person, Stella, calls me. She sets up the meeting, and I go to his place called the Hideaway."

"Oh my God, the Hideaway!!!!" he shrieks. And for a moment I think we might have lost him. The fact that Raymond couldn't plant this story somewhere, anywhere was just killing him. "Such a waste of good PR!" he fumes. "I could line up three blind script deals on this! Is it really called the Hideaway? You're making that up. Where's it located?"

"I don't know, Raymond. They blindfolded me before they took me there."

"What?!"

What I needed was a good distraction to get me off this phone call and back to work. It arrived as the front door opened and the nanny appeared with two exhausted children, one in tears, and the other pouting loudly.

"Got to go, Raymond. It's my shift to be mommy."

"Wait…Were you joking about the blindfold?"

I hung up, confident that he'd figure this one out on his own. I had bigger issues to deal with. Kathryn's best friend at pre-school had put a booger on her sweater, and she was crying inconsolably. Jacob wanted to shave his beautiful five-year-old hair into a Mohawk and was outraged no one agreed with him. It was one of those end-of-the-day meltdowns that are saved only for mothers. And especially for mothers who are writers. The nanny handed me Kathryn, quickly grabbed her purse, and made a dash for the door. All the problems of the world were now mine.

And then, the plot thickened.

The phone rang and I answered it not in the best of moods.

"Hello!" I shout over a television that's now blaring, a two-year-old that's sobbing, and a five-year-old slamming drawers in the kitchen as he searched for Daddy's hair clippers. "Jacob, don't you dare!" I yell as I lurch forward to pull him away from the dining room mirror with pinking shears in his hand.

"Hello?" the voice says softly, quizzically at the other end of the line.

I know that voice.

"Michael?"

"Darlene?"

"Michael?" I repeat, hoping I'm wrong.

"Darlene?"

I'm not.

"Michael!!!" shouts Jacob, who never misses a beat.

"Mike Call!!!" repeats Kathryn, always following the lead of her brother. Forgetting her tears now, and the booger incident, she joins Jacob who is clinging at my hip as I stand in the dining room with the phone pressed against my ear.

"Hi Michael!" I say, immediately turning my frazzled mommy voice into a happy, confident, professional screenwriter voice.

"Is it Michael Jackson?" Jacob asks in a loud stage whisper. Definitely the son of an actor.

I nod and put my finger up to my lips, showing the kids that they needed to be very quiet during this phone call.

"That's Michael Jackson, Katie!" Jacob says, leaning close to his sister's ear.

"Applejack?" she says hopefully, not able to pronounce Michael's full name.

I cover the mouthpiece and say "Shhh!" loudly to the kids.

Jacob turns to his sister, "Don't talk, Katie!"

"Okay," she says softly.

"How are you?" I ask Michael, nonchalantly.

"I really enjoyed our last meeting," he says softly.

"Me too!" I tell him.

I try to move down the hallway to my office. But Jacob

is clinging to my side, dragging Kathryn along with him. Clearly, this was going to be a group phone call.

"Do you know if we're meeting this week?" I ask.

"Stella handles all of that. She'll call you with all the information."

"Right! Good!" I say, trying to shake loose of the kids. But Jacob and Kathryn just cling to me tighter, like I'm the Dumbo ride at Disneyland.

"Let me talk to him!" Jacob whispers.

"Applejacks!" Kathryn shouts. And I cover the mouth-piece quickly.

"I wanted to give you my personal number," Michael says. "The one at the Hideaway and the one I have at the Ranch. I have to keep changing them all the time, and I wanted to make sure you have them in case you need to reach me."

"Oh right, great!" I say, madly racing back into the dining room, and searching for a pen, a pencil, anything to write with. Kathryn giggles loudly as I drag her along with me. I find a box of crayons on the living room table, rip one out, and search desperately for paper. I grab a coloring book.

"Mine! Mine!" shouts Kathryn, and rips it out of my hand.

At the other end of the line, Michael starts to rattle off several numbers, and I quickly write them down on top of the coffee table.

"Mommy!!!!" gasps Jacob.

Kathryn loves the idea, picks up a crayon and joins me, scribbling over the wood.

"Katie!!!!" Jacob wails, clearly feeling the need to play parent now since Mommy wasn't doing the job. He grabs the crayon out of his sister's hand, and she bites him. Jacob screams and then grabs Kathryn's hair, throwing her to the ground.

"You can call me day or night," Michael says, and I clamp my hand tightly over the mouthpiece so he won't hear the screams and wailings now coming from Jacob and Kathryn fighting on the floor.

"Anytime you have some ideas, and you want to run through them with me, just give me a call. You don't have to wait until we have a meeting scheduled if you want to talk. This project is very important to me. I'm very excited about it."

I have the phone in the crook of my neck as I use both hands to keep the kids separated from one another.

"That's great, Michael. I feel the same," I assure him, as Jacob and Kathryn both cry in my arms.

"Are those your kids?" Michael asks.

"How'd you guess?" I say, as both kids wail loudly.

Michael laughs, "See you at the next meeting!"

I couldn't wait.

I actually *wanted* to get out of the house.

10
An Invitation
Too Big to Turn Down

Neverland filled up my nights.

Since I couldn't drive myself to my office, I had to work at home and around my kids' schedule. The best hours to write were when they were in bed. When David was off at rehearsals, and when the house was finally quiet, that was when Peter, Hook, the Lost Boys, and Tinkerbell came into my life.

In his opening pages of *Peter Pan*, J.M. Barrie wrote that he had no recollection of ever having written the story. When screenwriting goes well, it can feel that same way: almost effortless. You become lost in the tale; words simply tumble out, and you, as the inspired writer, hurry to catch them on paper. Barrie found his inspiration in the form of four young boys that he had befriended in Kensington Gardens in London, a place he often visited with his big St. Bernard named Porthos. The adventures he had with those children became the heart and soul of *Peter Pan*. The imaginary games they played involving pirates, faeries, and fantasy, distilled through Barrie's style and wit, metamorphosed into his characters and story.

My inspiration always comes from music. I need it to write, to visualize the scenes in my mind. Every film has its soundtrack, and until I find the music for each project I work on, I'm not able to see the film playing out in my imagination.

I was having trouble finding the music for Neverland. Michael had sent over his *Thriller* tape, and as I watched it I started seeing Peter Pan in Michael's movements: the way he struts, and challenges, his boyishness, and his passion. But his music was too contemporary, and I couldn't find Neverland in its sound. What is the music of a place where you never age? Where the evil of Hook lives side by side with the innocence of Tinkerbell?

On my good nights, as I listened to Michael Jackson tracks on my headphones, and doodled Tinkerbell cartoons on my desk blotter, I was certain (like Michael) that we would make a film classic. On my bad nights, when I was intimidated by Barrie's brilliance, and when Peter and his friends refused to bring me into their circle, I was convinced I would never write another screenplay in my life. The bad nights were definitely outnumbering the good.

I was trying hard not to panic.

And then, Stella called.

"Michael's in town and wants to meet with you this weekend."

Now, I was beyond panicking. I didn't even know Michael was out of town. I assumed he was busy working at the recording studio day and night on his new album. Shows you how little I knew about my collaborator. One of the frustrating things about working on this project was not having a regular meeting schedule. It all depended on when Michael was available.

"I'd love to meet!" I lie to Stella.

I am not the best at micromanaging, or juggling family life with work, so weekends have always been off limits for writing. During the week, with a nanny available, I could be a part-time mommy. But on the weekend it was a 24-hour a day job, even with David helping me. On Saturdays and Sundays writing was the last thing on my mind, as my world turned into Happy Meals, G-Rated videos, timeouts, and tantrums.

"Sunday works," I lie again as I make the commitment.

As a freelance writer, I can make my own hours. But not every mommy in show business is so lucky. I once had a meeting with a film executive who had just given birth to her third baby. She had three within three years, and two of them were still in diapers. I asked her how she managed juggling work and her kids.

"I had a nervous breakdown," she had admitted. And she wasn't kidding—she had to be hospitalized. But there she was, this mommy/woman executive, back in her office again, looking calm, collected, and still working.

I asked her how she did it.

"Four nannies," she confessed with resignation. "Two full-time during the week, and two on the weekends around the clock."

I wondered if she remembered what her children looked like.

"I had to do it," she told me. "I don't want to resent my kids. When I spend time with them, I'm all theirs," she had said proudly with a smile. "Just not 24/7."

Somehow, this worked for her. It was her choice, but not one I wanted to make. At the moment, however, her decision seemed a much wiser (and healthier) one than being split down the middle by my kids' needs and the demands of Project M.

At least Michael and I were only meeting at night.

"Our usual time at 9 p.m?" I ask Stella.

"Oh no, honey. Not at the Hideaway."

"We're not meeting at the Hideaway?"

"Michael wants you to come out to the Ranch."

The Ranch?

"He wants to show you Neverland."

Oh shit.

Chills went up my spine, and not in a good way.

Neverland was two hours up the coast and another hour inland. And that's only one way. Doubling that meant a lot of hours traveling by myself, and being away from the house. It was something I hadn't had to do for years, not since a research trip for a Motown project took me all the way to Houston. And I almost had to cancel that trip.

Two days before I was scheduled to leave, I had a major panic attack, realizing I just couldn't do it. Houston was so far away, and I was terrified to fly and equally terrified to spend an entire week in a strange new place. I had a total emotional meltdown, and I was one phone call away from quitting the job. Luckily, a friend of mine (who was like a brother) volunteered to drive me all the way to Texas. Non-stop, 36 hours. In a Cadillac.

"I'll only do it if it's a Cadillac," he had insisted.

He didn't want to spend 36 hours of non-stop driving cramped into some small import. He was tall so he needed the extra leg space, and I needed to do research in Texas. So we hit the road and 36 hours later, we drove up to the Houston Hyatt in a pink Cadillac (the only one available) at 2:30 in the morning. Bleary-eyed and unwashed, we got there with plenty of time to spare for a noon lunch meeting. But I was so phobic the entire week I was in Houston my friend had to escort me to all of my meetings just to make sure I wouldn't lock myself in my hotel room and refuse to come out. At 6'3" and tipping the scales at almost 300 lbs, he was an intimidating force. The producer was certain he was my bodyguard and that my family had ties to the mafia. Better she thought that than knew the real truth: that I was agoraphobic.

After that Houston trip, I made myself a promise never to take another script assignment that involved traveling. I had enough trouble trying to get to a meeting in town. How was I supposed to handle one in another area code?

Impossible.

Of course I don't say that to Stella.

"Sounds wonderful!" I once again fib.

Lying gets easier the more you do it.

"If this was anybody but Michael Jackson, I'd cancel," I later admit nervously to David. "But I can't do that without jeopardizing this project. Plus, I really want to see Neverland!"

We are sitting on the front stoop watching Jacob pedal his two-wheeler down the sidewalk a few houses and then back to us again. Still using training wheels, he's anxious for David to remove them so he can take that next step to becoming a "big boy." Kathryn wiggles impatiently in my arms while sitting on my lap. She wants to race after her brother; in her eyes he's already "big," and doing everything she can't do yet.

At the end of the block (a very long block to my eyes), I see the tall concrete walls of the studio just across Santa Monica Blvd. My office is beyond those walls, just a few hundred feet. But in my world it seems as far away as Michael's Neverland. They are both two places too difficult to reach.

"I can do the meeting, but it's all that traveling by myself," I explain to David, hating the fact that my life is so complicated by this.

"I can drive you," David says simply, as though it's no big deal. In my world it *is* a big deal, but not in his, or in anybody else's. It always amazes me that people can just go places and do things and not have to figure out how they'll get there or if they can get there at all. "I'll drop you off, and drive into Solvang to wait for you. I can even bring the kids. We could spend the day there, having "appelskivers,"" he says to Kathryn, using a Danish accent.

Kathryn laughs as David takes her into his arms, and she stops her squirming.

"App...skeeves!!!" Tripped up by the word, Kathryn just claps instead.

"I can come back and pick you up when the meeting is finished," says David.

I reach out and take his hand. What has seemed so frightening and problematic David has now made doable. As he always does. He's become my safety person, a lifeline to the world.

If you're afraid to leave the house, and you're lucky enough to have someone like David in your life, you know that when he's with you, you're safe wherever you are, that there will always be a hand to hold when it gets too terrifying outside, and you need to go home. David makes it much easier for me to try to take those steps back into the world. I know when the fear is just too much, I can always tell him, and he'll never force me to go forward when I need to go back.

I call Stella the next day.

"I forgot to get directions to Neverland," I tell her, as casually as I can. "My husband is driving me there, and he knows the area. But is there an address?" I ask in all innocence.

"Oh no, honey," Stella says, stunned by the idea. "You have to come alone."

"He'll just drop me off," I explain, trying not to sound anxious. "He'll go into Solvang for the day, and when the meeting is over he'll come back to pick me up. At the gate," I add quickly. "He doesn't even have to come inside the property."

"Michael wouldn't like that," she tells me, ominously. "He doesn't know your husband, and it would make him feel very uncomfortable."

Michael would be uncomfortable? Lady, if you only knew.

Of course, I don't tell that to Stella.

"We'll have the studio send a car for you," she says with a smile in her voice. "Michael's really looking forward to this meeting! He can't wait!"

"Great!" I say, cheerfully.

What else could I say?

11
Off to Neverland

Steven's car wasn't available for the weekend, so the studio hired one from a local limousine service for the trip to Neverland. The new Town Car appeared in my driveway early Sunday morning like Cinderella's coach arriving to take me to the ball.

Wayne, the driver, a mountain of a man with blonde rock-star-length hair and a pierced ear, pulls himself out of the driver's seat to greet me.

"Hey!" he says with a Hollywood smile as he searches pocket after pocket in his uniform-black slacks for my information.

I introduce myself to save him the time.

"Cool!" he says, and it won't be the last time he says it. He flashes me those impeccably white teeth again as he holds open the car door, and I climb inside.

Once he's behind the wheel, his eyes catch mine in the mirror.

"Where are we going?" he asks, and he's not kidding.

I'm already nervous, and Wayne isn't helping.

"Don't you know?" I ask, a little shocked.

"I was half-asleep when they called," he explains. "I wasn't supposed to work today. I've got Laker tickets," he tells me, not looking thrilled not to be using them.

"You have no idea at all?" I ask him, incredulously.

"I can call the office and ask," he explains. "It's somewhere north, I remember that much," he admits.

Not the most reassuring answer.

Luckily, I had asked Stella for directions, and I knew the way. I was born in Santa Barbara, forty-five minutes south of the Santa Ynez Valley, so I had a pretty good idea where Neverland Ranch was located. I knew where we were going, and I could get us there easily.

Wayne, however, seemed clueless.

He wasn't making me feel too confident about stepping out of the house. But at this point there was no turning back; I couldn't cancel this meeting. I had a choice to make: to totally freak out or to have a little fun. Freaking out never helps agoraphobia, but a sense of humor can sometimes make you forget the fear.

"Just get on the 101 and head north," I tell him. "Guess where we're going."

"Cool!" he says, excited to be playing this game.

Nothing shakes up this guy.

We're quiet for most of the drive, but two hours into our trip, as we make our way through Santa Barbara, I ask Wayne if he has any idea yet where we're heading.

"Frisco?" he asks.

"Closer." I tell him.

I decide to give him a little hint: I say that I'm a screen-writer, and that he's driving me to a meeting about a film I'm writing.

"Cool!"

Judging by his language, I'm guessing that limo driver isn't his only job.

"I'm a musician," he volunteers.

"Cool!" I say, using the word for the day. "My meeting is with a musician," I add, giving him a big clue.

"Way cool!" he says, excited by the possibilities. "Is it Kenny Loggins? He lives up here."

"Nope, not Kenny Loggins."

While Wayne hemmed and hawed, trying to figure out where the hell he was driving me, I watched the stunning views of California's Central Coast outside my window. The freeway cut through the land as the Santa Ynez Mountains sloped to the ocean; on one side majestic foothills stood watch, and on the other side, the blue expansive waters of the Pacific stretched out to the horizon. It had rained the day before and the grasslands of the foothills were lush and starting to fill with orange California poppies while yellow mustard grass grew wild and untamed in fields where cattle grazed.

The Santa Barbara Channel Islands, often shrouded in fog and hidden by their distance from the shore, revealed them-selves in the clean, sweet air, a gift from yesterday's storm.

Like driftwood left behind on the sands, the sight of the islands intrigued, beckoned, and took hold of the imagination. My eyes scanned the rocky shores and pampas grassed bluffs, seldom seen from the mainland 90 miles away, as my mind searched for the beginnings of Neverland in the islands just off our coast.

It's hard to pinpoint when a film first takes hold of a screenwriter, and you begin to live with it day and night. One moment there is just you (and the people that populate your world), and then when a film begins to grow inside of you, it becomes a part of everything you do. Every waking moment is filtered through it, every word uttered, every action taken, sometimes consciously, and sometimes not. A conversation overheard in a coffee shop, a friend's laughter, a stranger's gait, a goodnight kiss from your child; all of the moments that make up a life find their way into the imagination, slipping into other faces and other bodies, taking on another life in a different story, unseen except by one person: the screenwriter. This is how *Peter Pan* came to me (as it must have come to Barrie): in little moments from my life, like the islands just outside the Town Car as we drove up the coast to Michael's Neverland.

"Michael Jackson!!!" Wayne suddenly shouts, as we turn off the 101 Freeway and onto the 154 Highway that snakes through the Santa Ynez back country.

"Bingo!" I say.

"He's not going to actually be there, is he?!!!"

"He better be. We have a meeting."

"No way!!!"

I pray he doesn't swerve off the road in excitement as I give him the rest of the driving instructions to Neverland Ranch.

"Am I going to drive you all the way into the Ranch?!" he asks, breathlessly.

"I'd hate to think I'd have to hike to the front door."

We are in the middle of nowhere and hiking is what people do out here. Except for a rustic boarding school for the privileged children of the well to do, Michael's Neverland Ranch is completely isolated in the fertile footprint of Figueroa Mountain. Turning off Highway 154, we head up Lookout Mountain Road where we reach a private entrance that leads to a small guardhouse next to a wooden gate.

The large gentleman at the gate, with massive shoulders of a linebacker, comes out to meet the car. Wayne obediently (but nervously) rolls down his window, the back windows, the front passenger window, and accidentally turns on the wipers that scrape across the dry windshield noisily.

I give the guard my name, and he disappears back into the guardhouse to phone it in. While I wait for clearance, I notice a sign prominently displayed that reads like a release form, stating that no photographic devices are allowed inside without written permission. I haven't finished reading it before the guard hands a clipboard through the back window and asks for my signature. It's a release form like the one posted at the gate. Wayne has to sign one too, and he is beyond impressed.

"This is so worth missing a Lakers game for!!!"

Magically, the wooden gates in front of us part slowly. On one side are the carved letters spelling "Neverland," and on the other side "Once Upon A Time."

"Cooooool!" Wayne mutters, as he accelerates slowly, and the Lincoln Town Car pushes forward, leaving this world and entering a fairy tale.

The road ahead of us curves into the countryside that's filled with ancient oaks, lush Manzanilla, and the promise of adventure. For the first time, I understand what Wendy must have felt as she soared above the clouds, awaiting the first glimpse of the mystical island called Neverland. Wayne and I are silent, too frightened to break this magical spell of anticipation or to awaken one another from some strange, but wonderful dream we're sharing.

Suddenly, appearing in the distance, a massive Tudor-style house looms at the end of the road—like Mandalay, mysterious and shrouded, not by fog, but by a forest of Sycamore trees. Spread out in front of the manor is a blanket of blossoming flowers all yellow, purple, and orange that frame the lush green patches of immaculately manicured lawns. As we move closer, we see a large lagoon, curving around the edge of the grounds, bordered by manmade babbling brooks that spill over river rocks, cascading into the body of water. Two tall fountains spout majestically at the corners of the lagoon; there are ducks and graceful swans skimming its surface.

As we approach closer, the road becomes a driveway that circles in front of the house and perched waiting there is an antique carriage with its ornately costumed horse, and a real-live coachman in a top hat and tails. Whip in hand, dressed in formal riding gear with perfectly black-polished boots, he sits motionless like the brass statues of playing children that cover these grounds everywhere you look.

Huddled around a cobblestone bridge that spans the lagoon, the lifelike statues of a group of children are posed, bending down, and dipping brass hands into the blue water of the flowing creeks. A boy in a bowler hat, his golden metallic skin shining from the noontime sun, stands barefoot, with fishing pole in hand. Everywhere you look, there is beauty and innocence personified, frozen in a kind of timeless perfection.

Wayne pulls the car up to the brick steps of the house and parks. For a moment, we just sit there, frozen like the bronze children outside our window, not wanting to break this spell that's captured both of us. A faint sound of music seems to be coming from somewhere, and as Wayne opens the door for me, I step out of the car, and the music swells, growing louder. I look around for the source, but the music mysteriously is all around us, filling the air like some soundtrack for the scene that we've just entered.

I walk up the brick steps of the house, leaving my world behind me. I am Wendy, Cinderella, and Alice through the looking glass. I am truly somewhere I don't belong. I am enchanted and swept away as I knock on the large, carved wooden door of Neverland's picturesque mansion.

12
A Day at the Ranch

Martin from the Philippines opens the door.

Fortyish and petite, he is soft-spoken and overly gracious. With a thick accent, he's timidly subservient as though he's afraid he might make a mistake and be banished from the kingdom.

My name is barely out of my mouth before he greets me.

"Oh yes! Come in, please. Mr. Jackson is expecting you."

I step into the foyer, and my eyes adjust to the sudden darkness of the rich tones of dark wood in the entrance of the house. The walls are trimmed in oak paneling, and the floors (I will learn later) are the well-worn wood planks from an 18th century chateau that was dismantled in France and flown to the U.S. by the house's first owner. High above is an elegant chandelier, all brass and punctuated by tiny lights.

In the center of the foyer, a hand-carved staircase leads up to an open-view second floor. A sycamore tree logo (from the pre-Michael days when this was called Sycamore Valley Ranch) is carved into its banister, and high above it are the rough-hewn Tudor-style roof beams. I can't help but think of Henry VIII: this is certainly a King's palace, if only for the King of Pop.

Now that I'm inside, Martin doesn't seem to know what to do with me.

"Will you … I must … Excuse me … Perhaps you will sit in the library?"

I look to Martin wordlessly for help: I have no idea where the library is located. Hopefully, he'll point it out.

"Oh yes! I will show you. This way, please …"

Either Michael has very few visitors here, or Martin must be new. He seems rattled and unsure, but I follow him anyway as he leads me across the entrance hall and into what I hope will be the library.

It is.

I walk into a room that would be the envy of any writer: Hundreds of leather bound books from floor to ceiling are neatly tucked into their built-in wooden bookcases that line the walls. Martin asks me to take a seat, and scurries out of the library while I settle into a leather armchair, and take in the ambience of the room.

Surrounded by so many books, I feel sheltered here, and (for a moment) not so phobic. There is a quiet serenity in this room that's palpable. Silence is a rare commodity in a home with two small children and in a career that demands 24-hour attendance; this sense of calm is rarely felt. The books are comforting, but the view outside is even more peaceful.

Beyond the thick beveled glass of a bow window is the most beautiful giant oak tree that I have ever seen. With its thick trunk and gnarled branches reaching skyward, it sits on its own patch of grass like a guardian of the house. Underneath its limbs is a redwood lounge chair, and beyond, the view stretches out pristine and limitless: the lagoon with its cascading waters, gardens in full bloom, and the green-coated Santa Ynez Mountains. While inside the library, the music of *Tristan and Isolde* plays softly throughout the room.

Almost as if on cue, a deer magically appears, moving sprite-like along one of the brooks, to pause for a drink of water and to stare eye to eye with me through the window's glass wall. For a moment I wonder if it's even real—if by chance Disney imagineers are at work, unseen behind the scenes, silently controlling this magical paradise with electronic push buttons and wireless animation.

Michael comes into the room, breaking the spell, looking flustered and even more nervous than Martin.

"I'm so sorry, Darlene..."

"Why?"

"We're supposed to meet, but I don't know how that's going to happen..."

He seems skittish as he meets me in the doorway, and then starts to lead me out of the library, down the hallway towards the living room.

"Is there a problem?" I ask.

"I have a visitor, and he won't leave!" he says, sounding

totally exasperated as he guides me through the beautifully appointed living room with its roughly hewn oak floors and a grand piano covered with silver framed photos of Michael, his family, and numerous celebrities and dignitaries.

"I don't know what to do!" Michael says, as he leads me next into the largest kitchen I've ever seen in my life.

The room is filled with butcher block islands covered with Portuguese blue painted tiles, double fireplaces are built into the far brick wall, and a bank of windows overlook the rolling foothills beyond Neverland. A cook is hard at work along with several domestics, including Martin's wife, who is also middle-aged and petite. The sizeable room is filled with the smells of a meal being prepared or perhaps of one that's already been served.

We have barely entered the kitchen before Michael hands me a phone from behind a counter.

"Talk to Stella," he instructs, in a quiet, apologetic voice.

"Is this a bad time? Do you want me to come back?" I ask him.

He doesn't answer me. Too embarrassed to find the right words, his answer will be in Stella's voice at the other end of the phone.

"Jon Peters won't leave," she explains, letting out a little sigh.

Jon Peters is Sony Studios, or at least he runs it.

"He spent the weekend, and he was supposed to go home late this morning, but he's still there, and he doesn't seem to want to leave."

Who can blame him?

"There's a helicopter waiting for him, but he's just not leaving."

I look over at Michael who can barely make eye contact with me. It's obvious that he doesn't handle these kind of unpleasant moments in life: Stella does. I can't tell whether that's because he's a star and he pays people to handle problems for him, or if it's simply because he's just not good at this.

"What would you like me to do?" I ask Stella, even though Michael is standing right next to me, and we could easily be having this conversation ourselves. "Do you want me to leave?" I ask.

"No!" both Michael and Stella say, almost at the same time.

I feel like I'm dealing with a ventriloquist act.

"Michael really wants to meet with you," Stella explains so that Michael doesn't have to find the words—even though we're in the same room and so close to one another. I glance up at him, wondering if he'll at least look me in the eyes.

He does.

"Please stay," he mouths the words.

"Do you mind staying until I get Jon Peters out of there?" Stella asks.

"I'll stay here as long as you need," I tell her.

I look at Michael, and he's all smiles.

Something Stella doesn't need to tell me.

It will take several hours before the small red helicopter perched at the edge of the back property even starts up its engine. In the meantime, I am escorted to Michael's office (a separate cottage just off the main house) where I will be served lunch. I pass Wayne on my way there, and he's so excited because they are not only serving him lunch in the kitchen, he gets to hang out all day in the game room and video arcade bungalow that's filled with Pac-Man, Terminator, Star Wars, Air Hockey, and other electronic games.

"They're all free!!!" he exclaims as he disappears into the kitchen.

Plus, he's on the clock while he plays them.

In Michael's office, I set up camp and wait as the housekeeper serves me Tempura shrimp, a filet mignon steak sandwich, seasonal fresh fruit for dessert, and a pot of Chinese tea.

I'm amazed at how comfortable I feel here.

Not just because the surroundings are beautiful, or that if I need anything, all I have to do is ask. There's something else here in Neverland that's appealing to someone like me who never likes to leave the house. As I look through the windows of Michael's office it suddenly occurs to me that there aren't many people around. All of these beautiful acres of Neverland are the perfect buffer for keeping out the world.

An agoraphobic's paradise.

After lunch, Martin gives me a tour of the house.

I notice that there is absolutely no one in sight. The small staff discreetly stays hidden unless they're needed. Martin and I are alone as he takes me upstairs; our footsteps and the piped in classical music are the only sounds in the house.

We enter a large room that is filled entirely with toys, some are brand new, still in their boxes, and others are antiques and on display. The sight puzzles me; it looks like a small toy store. Martin says they are gifts for underprivileged youngsters and handicapped children that visit Neverland Ranch.

"Mr. Jackson loves the kids!" he explains. "Everything here in Neverland is for the kids. For them to have fun! And Mr. Jackson, he is like a kid himself. He plays with these toys— like a kid!!!"

"Keed" is how he says it. His accent is thick. His enthusiasm is off the charts; Martin is obviously thrilled and honored to be working at Neverland.

I peek into all the guest rooms and there on the nightstands are notepads and stationary with the "Neverland Valley" logo on them: A little boy dressed in footed pajamas (looking like a young Michael) sits all alone on the edge of a full moon. It reminds me of a hotel room and the stationary that comes with it. People seem to visit Neverland, but I'm having trouble picturing it as someone's home. It just doesn't look lived in, and there's something lonely about all these empty rooms.

After the house tour, Martin drives me around in Michael's black Mercedes, showing me more of the grounds while a cassette of classical music plays in the car. I learn that it permeates Neverland Ranch (from the moment you arrive), coming through speakers disguised as boulders or hidden in the trees. I listen to the cassette playing in the Mercedes as the beauty of Neverland passes outside the car's window, and I realize that finally I have found something I've been searching for.

Peter Pan's music.

13
A Kid in a Candy Store

By the time the little red helicopter lifts up at the back of Neverland and Jon Peters is heading home, it's 4:30 p.m. Michael and I still haven't met, and my confidence is starting to crumble. I've been away from the house for hours, and the nerves are kicking in. The distraction of Neverland's splendor isn't working on me anymore.

I want to go home.

But Michael and I still need to meet, and as the long afternoon shadows fall across the ranch, I can feel the edge of a panic creeping my way. To make matters worse, Stella called an hour ago to say that she was releasing Wayne and the car and that Michael's own personal chauffeur and limousine would take me home tonight.

Tonight?

I was supposed to be out of here by now and on my way home. I'll be lucky if I get back by midnight. And how could I possibly say goodbye to Wayne? I was just getting used to him. In a strange way, he had become my temporary safety person. We had bonded over a game of Pac-Man in the video arcade. But now he was heading back into the real world, leaving me all alone here in the fairy tale.

If I could only click my heels and get myself home.

Luckily, I don't have to wait much longer. Soon after the little red helicopter disappears over the mountains, I see Michael making his way up the path to the video arcade. I leave my Indiana Jones game mid-adventure to hurry outside and meet him.

He is filled with apologies for taking such a long time with Jon Peters, and he's anxious for us to watch Disney's *Peter Pan* together.

Martin appears (perfectly on cue), driving up in the black Mercedes. He scrambles out of the car, and over to the back door to open it for us.

"We don't need the car," Michael tells him.

Martin stops, turns, looks uncertain and confused.

"Come on, I'll show you the movie theater," Michael says to me, as he heads for a golf cart parked at the rear of the bungalow.

"I will drive?" Martin asks, as he hurries over to the golf cart.

"I can do it," Michael says, never slowing his stride.

Martin looks disoriented and not sure where he should go, what he should do, or what is needed from him. He bombards Michael with questions as he scurries along at his side: "Will you be needing the car? Should I bring the car to pick you up? Are you hungry? Should we prepare dinner?" Michael just shakes his head as he tries to ignore the assault, and climbs into the golf cart.

"Come on, Darlene," he says.

I hurry to climb in next to him as he turns the key, and we pull away quickly, leaving Martin behind us, looking totally lost.

"Oh my gosh, he is so stupid," Michael says softly, clearly bothered by Martin's insecurity and clinginess. He presses his foot down harder on the gas pedal, and we head deeper into the grounds.

Classical music plays from unseen speakers in the trees.

"The music is beautiful!" I say.

"I love classical music!"

"There was something playing in the car that was perfect for Peter's music. Martin didn't know the name of it."

Michael just shakes his head in contempt. "He's so stupid!"

"It was very lyrical!"

Should I try to hum it, I wonder?

"Ralph Vaughan Williams," Michael says, immediately.

He saves me the embarrassment of humming off tune for the King of Pop.

"'A Pastoral Symphony,'" he adds, naming it.

I'm impressed he knows without even hearing a note of it.

"It's beautiful!" I tell him.

"It's Neverland!" he says, smiling and nodding his head knowingly.

Neverland's movie theatre is next to a huge tree house and play area that overlooks a dry creek bed in the middle of what seems like a forest of oaks. There is a rustic rope and wooden footbridge with a zip line to hold onto to slide through the trees. It's every child's perfect playground.

The movie theater itself is just as exciting. With its lobby filled with a refreshment counter containing every candy imaginable and stocked with bars of chocolate with Michael Jackson's image on the label, the smell of freshly popped popcorn adds to the ambiance of what looks like a small town movie house.

"Take whatever you want," Michael encourages me. "You want some popcorn, or a coke?" he asks, and with a wave of his hand he lets me wander behind the counter like a kid literally in a candy shop. He's Willy Wonka in the Chocolate Factory, and I fight the urge to snatch up as many samples that will fit into my large workbag.

Filling up the lobby of the theatre are several glass-enclosed animated dioramas, each with a scene from a Disney classic like *Cinderella*, and *Snow White*.

"I have one from *Peter Pan* in my bedroom," Michael tells me excitedly. "I'll show it to you later."

The movie theatre itself is state of the art with everything electronically controlled. Two glass-walled rooms upstairs at the back of the theatre, each equipped with a large bed covered with stuffed animals, have been specially designed for children who are too ill to sit in the theatre and watch films. Michael explains to me that children with terminal diseases or specialized health needs are invited to Neverland so they can watch the latest released films, and have a day when they can just feel like "normal kids."

"They love it!" he tells me, thrilled that he can make them forget their problems, if only for one day.

We take our seats near a console so that Michael can electronically control the sound. We are there to watch Disney's *Peter Pan*, but Michael wants me to see the two *Kick the Can* episodes of *The Twilight Zone*. First, we watch the black and white original, and then he screens Spielberg's version from his feature film. Michael talks all through the Spielberg version. "Why did he change that? He changed it, you see? It's not as good—he changed it and the old one was better."

After both have played, he shakes his head.

"There's no heart in Steven's version," he says. "Don't you agree?"

Before I can answer, the phone on the console next to him lights up, and he reaches over to it. His face brightens when he hears who is at the other end, and then he lowers his voice with concern and comforting.

"I know, I heard. It's shocking. How are you doing?" he says.

Phone calls interrupt meetings all the time in show business. As a screenwriter, you just get used to it, and do what you always do: wait. Wait to continue the story meeting. Wait to continue your pitch. Wait to get notes from producers, directors, the studio. It always feels like a show of power. The screenwriter has none and is reminded of this the longer the phone call goes on. The call that Michael is taking at the moment sounds as though it could be a long one as he tries to comfort the person at the other end of the phone.

"I have to take this," he whispers to me, covering up the mouthpiece. "It's Liz," he adds, as though that explains why the need to talk.

Liz meaning Elizabeth Taylor: She and Michael are the best of friends. Thank God my mother fills me in on everything she reads in the National Enquirer.

So here I sit next to Michael Jackson who is talking...no, actually consoling Elizabeth Taylor. And how can I not eavesdrop on this conversation?

"He was old, and he had heart problems. I know, it's still shocking, I know how close you were, but it happens. He was old," Michael says, and turns to look at me. "Someone she was very close to just passed away," he explains to me in a whisper, again covering the mouthpiece.

Malcolm Forbes has died and he was a close friend of Elizabeth Taylor. I remember this from articles in issues of the Star that my mother had quoted for me. On the phone with Michael, Liz is brokenhearted, and I wonder, "Do I get up and give them some privacy? Or do I just sit there and wait, awkwardly, as every writer does when a meeting is interrupted by a phone call?" Choices like this they don't teach you in film school. Luckily, I didn't go to film school, and my instincts tell me I should check out the lobby again.

I decide I need a Coke and leave the room.

Back in the lobby, I play with the dioramas and grab a chocolate bar with Michael's dancing image on the label. I unwrap it, and there is his image again, molded in milk chocolate. I wonder how many chocolate bars I can take home with me? Two, ten? Too bad I left my workbag in the library; I could stash a dozen.

Michael seeks me out in the lobby, after the long phone call with Elizabeth is finished. He walks me back into the theatre so we can begin to watch Disney's *Peter Pan*.

"I'm sorry about the phone call," he says to me, apologetically. "Liz is a wreck right now."

What I witnessed was a tender, personal moment between the best of friends. But for someone like me, not a member of their world, it's difficult to look past their notoriety and to see them just as everybody else. How many people have their images on a chocolate bar? Or live in such splendor? Everywhere I look around Neverland, I'm only reminded that Michael is a celebrity.

It's hard to think of him as anything else.

It's dark outside when the film finishes, and we emerge from the movie theatre. Neverland has been transformed: thousands of twinkling little white lights outline the large tree house and rope bridge, strung among the branches of the surrounding grove of giant oaks.

"Oh Michael!" I say breathlessly when I first catch sight of all of the lights. "How beautiful!!!"

"What?" he asks, in all innocence.

"All the lights! They're so stunning!"

"Oh yes," he says quietly, already seemingly used to the sight; too familiar with its beauty to be thrilled anymore.

We walk back to the house, and Martin suddenly appears in the doorway.

"Can I get you anything, Mr. Jackson? Something to eat? Something to drink?"

He hovers tight at our heels, and Michael waves him away like some unwanted night insect. Obediently, Martin disappears as quickly as he made his entrance.

"Let me show you something," Michael says to me, as we cross through the living room, heading for a bedroom just off the foyer. "It's in my room," he tells me, as he leads the way.

Once again I find myself in Michael Jackson's bedroom.

I am surprised by how cluttered it is. His bed is unmade, and the room is filled with books, magazines, games, knickknacks, and just plain "stuff." Nothing is neatly tucked away like in the other rooms of the house. It reminds me of my son's bedroom that is filled with toys here and there, games he's played with but hasn't put away. It looks so different than the other rooms in the house. This is a room where someone obviously lives; life goes on here. It's messy, and disorganized, fascinating, and comfortable.

Among the untidiness is another glass-enclosed diorama displaying a scene from Disney's *Peter Pan*. Michael eagerly shows it to me, turning it on. At the press of a button, the scene comes alive three dimensionally, and one of the songs from the film plays, "I can fly, I can fly, I can fly!"

"I have another copy of *Peter Pan* I want to show you. The pictures are so beautiful!" Michael says to me, excitedly.

He searches through piles of books for it, having trouble finding it at first. And while he is looking, I glance over at something that first caught my eye as I walked into the room: a framed painting of the Blessed Heart of Jesus hangs above his bed. I don't know why, but I am surprised to see it in this room. Its presence here makes Michael for the moment seem just like everyone else: vulnerable and uncertain. In need of something bigger than himself.

For the first time, I see past the celebrity.

Michael finally finds the book he's been looking for, and we sit together on the edge of his bed as he shares the pages of it with me. It's *Peter Pan in Kensington Gardens*, the original 1906 edition with illustrations by Arthur Rackham. They are famous illustrations, and Michael proudly shows them off to me, page by page, each one more magnificent than the one before it. It is a priceless first edition, and I suddenly realize that the copy of *Peter and Wendy* that I gave to him is nothing compared to this book.

I spent a lot of money (at least in our family budget) to buy that book for Michael, but holding this illustrated first edition in my hands I now understand that a lot of money to me is nothing in Michael's world. And yet, when I gave him the gift, he thanked me graciously and never said he already owned not only the book, but also a better version of it.

The Blessed Heart hanging on the wall, the messiness of his room, and his unspoken kindness makes me like Michael even more.

Not as a celebrity, but as a person.

14
Tea and Shortbread
in the Library

We settle in the library, and slowly we begin to work.

Michael loves books and seems to surround himself with them, not just here in the library but in his bedroom too.

"I have every book ever written about Peter Pan, and J.M. Barrie!" Michael says proudly.

I've brought him a book called *Faeries*, and as I pull it from my workbag, Michael's eyes light up. I hand him the beautifully illustrated over-sized edition, and he flips through the pages eagerly. The book explains how communities of faeries live in hollow hills, and I suggest to him that perhaps Tinkerbell is part of a community like this. There's something magical and powerful about faeries that might help drive our plot.

"Like what?" Michael asks, curious like a child.

"Pixie dust," I suggest with a smile. "When faeries fly, their wings produce pixie dust."

"It's what helps children fly," Michael says, stating it like a fact of life.

"Barrie added pixie dust to his play because too many children who saw the early productions were jumping off their beds trying to fly, and they were getting hurt," I tell Michael. "That's why Barrie added pixie dust to the later productions. Without it, children wouldn't think they could possibly fly, so they stopped jumping off their beds to try."

Michael giggles, "Kids!"

"So we have this wonderful theatrical device—pixie dust, and I think we should really use it." I point to an illustration in the *Faeries* book. "Fairies live together in a hollow hill, and we can show that in Neverland. Can you imagine all the pixie dust that would be in that hill? Visually, it could be magical!"

"I like that," Michael says, speaking softly. "We have to create something that Captain Hook wants so badly…"

Suddenly, Martin enters the room, interrupting as he noisily pushes a teacart loaded up with a full tea service and plates of freshly baked shortbread cookies. For a moment, the disruption breaks the spell, wrenching us out of our imaginations, and back to real life.

Michael waits Martin out, annoyed again by his presence. He looks away, everything shuts down inside of him. This isn't something he wants to handle; these inconveniences are someone else's job. I wonder as I watch Martin set up the tea service if he will still be here if I ever visit Neverland again. Or will Stella simply make another phone call, handling it so Michael doesn't have to be involved?

Michael and I wait silently as Martin finishes setting up the tea, and then pushes the cart, once again noisily, back out of the room.

It's dinnertime, and suddenly I'm feeling famished. I eagerly reach for the cookies and wonder if this means we won't be breaking for a meal. It doesn't seem to bother Michael. Once again he's not eating anything. The cookies sit in front of him, untouched, while mine quickly start to disappear. I've learned that if I don't eat, my blood sugar level drops, and I'm more prone to panic attacks. Skipping meals is not an option for me.

"It's not enough for Hook to battle Peter just out of revenge," Michael continues, finishing his thought after Martin has made his exit from the room.

"Mm hmm," I say, my mouth filled with shortbread cookies.

"Hook wants Neverland completely. Like being King of a country."

He thinks for a moment while I continue to wolf down the cookies and tea.

"That pixie stuff, what you were talking about, I like that." He reaches over to an end table, picking up a beautiful wooden boxed game. Turning it from side to side, a steel ball rolls within, and he plays with it.

"Does Hook want to fly?" he asks.

It's great character motivation, and it's the reason I suggested all the pixie dust. Pirates are always looking for treasure, and if Hook wants to fly, this can be the treasure he's looking for. I was hoping Michael would see the connection. And he does.

"We've got to make Hook reallllllly vicious!" he suddenly announces, setting down the wooden game box. He begins to slap out a little rhythm on the side of his leg with his hand. His foot starts tapping on the floor, as he begins to build a scene.

"When they get to Neverland, you see these beautiful mermaids," Michael says, giggling softly. "And Hook should end up capturing all the mermaids, and keeping them in his cellar, without water. You see them slowly dying. They're turning white, or whatever…What do you think of something like this?"

Well, we weren't really discussing mermaids, so I hesitate. He's taking us off in another direction, and I have to bring him back. But how do I do that without shooting down his ideas?

Maybe he needs a break? Maybe he needs to eat. I don't know how he can spend all day meeting with Jon Peters, go right into discussing *Peter Pan* for hours, and then do a dance rehearsal at 9 p.m. after I leave. Without a break? Without even touching his cookies and tea?

"There should be different areas of Neverland that we see, and one of them is the mermaid lagoon."

"That'd be excellent!" Michael says, excitedly.

I've hooked him with mermaids, now I take him in another direction.

A new plot point.

"Near the Mermaid Lagoon is a section of Neverland where you can look through this mist and see the real world. It's a place that Peter has always told the Lost Boys never to go near."

I pause, and Michael waits, looking with the same anticipation that I've seen in the eyes of my children when I tell them a bedtime story.

"You know as you grow older, you start to explore, and move away from your parents, moving more into the world."

I'm not sure Michael understands this about growing up. He hasn't lived a normal life: he's been a performer since he was a boy. Michael hasn't had to move out of his parent's house to go off to college or to take a job. Those milestones of growing up are something he hasn't experienced. I need to find a way to help him understand.

He likes the Lost Boys, and I use them as a hook.

"One by one the Lost Boys have wandered into these mists where they can see the real world. And they've left Neverland through here—this area that frightens Peter because he knows he will always lose his boys."

Michael is suddenly quiet.

"He always picks up new children because there are always needy children in the world. He goes out and rounds them up, bringing them to Neverland. But one by one the Lost Boys always get older, and they wander into the mists."

"That's nice," he says softly. "That's a threat of losing them," he adds, seeming to understand the loss.

"You see, the one thing Peter's never had to do before—he's never had to say goodbye to anybody…because the boys have always just left. They've always wandered off. Peter's never really had to say goodbye to anybody in his life. And I think that's why it breaks him up so much when he has to say goodbye to Wendy, Michael, and John. If we know that about Peter, that he's never had to say goodbye before, then our hearts are going to be breaking for him."

"Mm hm," he says, barely above a whisper.

Somehow I think I've reached him.

We are quiet for a very long time.

"The threat should always be there," Michael finally says. "Because it gives the story more heart. Like…'Please don't go, stay!'" He acts out the words, like Peter begging the children to stay with him. "There should always be the fact that they want to go back, they want to go home."

"That would be very difficult for Peter," I say softly.

Michael nods, understanding.

"Can Peter go back?" he suddenly asks.

"Back to the real world?"

"Mm hm."

"There's no way Peter can go back. Neverland's his home now."

"No way! He don't want to go back anyway!" he says, adamantly.

Silence fills the room again as Michael looks at me, challengingly.

"Do *you* like the real world?" he asks.

The question stuns me. I've never been asked a question like this before.

How does an agoraphobic answer this, I wonder?

"Do I like the real world?" I repeat.

I'm terrified by it, but I can't admit this to Michael.

He watches me and waits for my answer.

How I answer him is important. We have a connection, Michael and I: our love for *Peter Pan*. I don't want to do anything that might jeopardize it.

Peter Pan is about the fear of growing up. Casting aside childhood and going into the world of adults. For me, growing up meant putting away my tomboy ways. Everything that Peter Pan represents, the adventures he had, his confidence, and his independence is what I had built my childhood around. Wendy was boring but not Peter. Growing up and giving up this sense of power I had as a little girl to become a woman did not sound like much fun to me at all. As a child I was fearless, and the world seemed so inviting. But now I have so many fears keeping me inside. And yet, there are times while in the safety of my house I long to be a part of the world again, to move with that same sense of confidence that Peter has.

I wonder what it is about growing up that frightens Michael.

There is something in the way he's asked me if I like the world that tells me that he doesn't like it, that in some ways he's as uncomfortable in it as I am.

"Sometimes I like the real world," I say softly.

I think of my children and the love of my husband. And becoming a writer to relive those adventures of my childhood, even if they're only in my imagination or on a script's page. These are the things that make up for whatever is keeping me inside.

"There are aspects of the world that are …"

Dare I say wonderful and risk alienating Michael?

"… not so bad."

I chicken out for the sake of the project.

Michael is quiet for a long time, and I'm not sure it's the answer he wanted to hear from me. The world through his eyes seems dark and hurting, and I think he needs me to confirm that. When I don't, that fragile link between us is broken. I search for a way to reconnect with him once again.

"Do you think there's a conflict in Peter?" I ask. "If he isn't from the real world, but the Lost Boys are, does Peter know they have to go back some day?"

"That's the thing," he says, without pause. "It bothers him, and he cries about it by going off into the forest. Just thinking about it, that he's going to lose them. That they may not want to stay, and they will grow up. And Peter… See, I think Peter is a very lonely person."

I look at him, not sure of what to say. I wonder if he's talking about Peter, or maybe talking about himself.

"Very lonely," he repeats it again, softly. "And he wants friends so badly. He wants someone to stay. So he takes them not only for their own good, but for them to keep him company… And it hurts, really hurts."

"I think Peter has never shown that pain to anybody…" I say quietly. "He'll go off into the forest, and he'll let the animals see it. But he never shows it to the boys,"

"Never shows it," he speaks almost too softly to be heard.

"He'd never show that pain to anyone… But you know maybe Wendy sees it."

"Mm hm."

"I think that hurts her that Peter is in pain. That Peter is lonely."

We stop talking for a moment, and the only sound in the room is the tape quietly turning in the handheld recorder sitting on the table. I wonder in the silence if we really have been talking about Peter Pan at all, or if that line between actor and character has been crossed? At what point does an actor become the role? Or the role becomes the actor?

"'S'cuse me," Michael suddenly announces. "I have to tinkle!'"

He heads quickly for the bathroom in the hall.

And the meeting is on hold while Michael goes off to tinkle.

15

Giggles, a Sweet Tooth, and an Unzipped Zipper

When Michael is finished with his bathroom break, he disappears down the hallway and comes back into the library with both hands filled with Jolly Roger candies. He sets some on the table in front of me and takes the rest for himself, while settling into his armchair. Kneeling down on the seat, and tucking his legs under him, he unwraps one of the candies and slides it into his mouth, sucking it. It's the first time I've seen him eat anything in these months that I've known him.

"I think it's very, very, very vital that we watch…" he begins, with renewed energy and vigor. "Not just watch, but study, and dissect it like a scientist… *The Wizard of Oz*, and *E.T.* Something about those two movies has and will effect generation upon generation. They have something, a quality that affects and touches everybody. And those elements that do that to the human soul we should make sure apply to our film. I mean those two films will live forever! It's very important as a study for us," he continues. "So that should be top priority, don't you think?"

He is always checking with me, always asking me my opinion. I never know whether he's testing me to make sure we're creatively in agreement or if he genuinely wants to hear my ideas. I'm more interested in keeping him happy at the moment, so I always say yes, and I always agree with him. That's easy to do at this stage of development: I don't have many ideas of my own yet.

I wonder what will happen between Michael and me once I do.

"We're walking a very delicate and fine line doing *Peter Pan*. It's very, very difficult," he explains. "We just have to push the right buttons in the human soul…we have to find those moments where we really get people. We must! Or else we haven't done our job."

He sucks on a Jolly Roger and the room grows quiet. I make a note of what he's said, and I wait for him to continue. But he remains silent as he sucks quietly on his candy, and I don't know if he's just thinking, or if we're finished for the night. I reach over for my own Jolly Roger on the table in front of me. Unwrapping it, I stall for time, looking over at the tape recorder to make sure the red record button is pushed down. It is. Michael watches me as I start to lick the candy, popping into my mouth.

I pick up the *Faeries* book.

"There's something in here about faeries not functioning well in bright light," I suggest. "You asked about Tinkerbell?"

"I like that! Bright lights…we can use that."

"Hook should have a lantern."

"Lanterns all around Tink. Torture her. Put her in the middle of them," he adds.

"Maybe torches of fire."

"How does he know this about Tink?" Michael asks.

"Tink maybe shrinks away from something in the house when they're with the kids. And then Peter says, 'Oh no, Wendy! Don't shine the flashlight on Tinkerbell!' Or 'A bright light can kill a faerie.' Something like that. 'Faeries are frightened by fire!'"

"So that's how the audience finds out," he nods and agrees with me.

"When Hook has her, maybe he goes to light his cigar, and suddenly he sees Tink flinch at … let's say, it's fire … She flinches as he lights his cigar. So whatever it is that's harmful to fairies, Hook sees this, and uses it against Tinkerbell."

"Oh no!" Michael suddenly gasps as he looks down at his lap.

What, I wonder? Is he disagreeing? Does he hate my idea?

"I didn't zip up my pants!!!" he says, incredulously.

I'm a little shocked.

"Oh you didn't?!" I say, with mock concern.

Is he kidding? I'm not about to look and confirm this.

I'm seriously wondering what is going on here. Michael has brought me into his bedroom twice, and now his fly is wide open. Why am I not concerned about this?

Suddenly, he starts to giggle uncontrollably.

That's why I'm not concerned.

When I'm with Michael I'm in the 3rd grade again. At that age when boys and girls chased each other, but the object of the game wasn't to get caught. Those days before hormones really kicked in. Everything about Michael seems preadolescent. I seriously doubt that calling attention to his open fly is his idea of flirting. Just as bringing me into his bedroom (twice) was as innocent as a nine-year-old's sleepover.

I'm willing to play along with his little game: Covering my eyes with my hands, I tell him quickly, "Ok, zip up your pants!"

We both really start to laugh now, as he zips up.

"Okay, I did it!" he lets me know so I can uncover my eyes.

He gives me a mischievous grin, and we go back to the story.

"I think there has to be a sweetness to Tinkerbell," I say, as we move right along.

"Totally," Michael agrees. "We have to do that big dying scene; the audience can't hate her."

"Steven was saying how Hook sort of seduces her. As a woman, you know, she sort of gives in, and joins with Hook."

"She wouldn't do that," he says adamantly. "She's crazy about Peter."

"I think she'd die for Peter. And she does die for Peter...I could just see Peter picking up a dying Tink. And his face as he talks to her," I say, playing with the scene a little.

"And Tink's light slowly dims. And Peter really gets mad."

Michael starts to act the scene, showing Peter's anger. "And he's ready for Hook now!"

"That's good!" I tell him as I make a note about the scene.

Michael unwraps another Jolly Roger and pops it into his mouth.

"Do you think it's possible to fly," he suddenly asks.

The question is another tricky one, and once again I have to be careful how I answer. Stalling for time, I repeat the question.

"Do I think it's possible to fly?"

Michael looks at me, much the same way my son does when he asks now (at age five) if I believe in Santa Claus.

"Sure!" I say in my most enthusiastic voice. How can I possibly tell him no?

His face fills with a great big smile.

"I was hoping you'd say that!"

"Really?" I say in my most innocent of voices.

As if I couldn't guess.

"I was gonna say: 'How could she write *Peter Pan* and not believe it's possible to fly?' he says. "I think it's totally possible! Humans just don't believe it cause we've been programmed to think in the ways of society."

"You accept rules of the world, and they're passed on from one generation to another, and if anybody dares to think differently, well, everybody tries to put that person down. And so it's, 'We can't fly! How can we possibly fly?!'"

"Mm hm" Michael nods, "Like Jesus."

I don't think he's suggesting Jesus can fly, but I'm not sure.

I reach for a sour cherry Jolly Roger on the table in front of me. Unwrapping it, I pop it into my mouth. Michael and I take a moment, sucking on our candies.

Suddenly, he begins to chuckle.

"What?" I ask.

"I'm thinking about faeries," he giggles.

"In the Disney film they're called pixies," I say.

"What should we call them?" he asks.

I bite down on my Jolly Roger, chewing it instead of sucking it.

"I was going to ask *you*," I tell him with a laugh, not willing to commit first.

We laugh a moment together, understanding the unspoken dilemma.

"You know, people call gays faeries," he tells me, like we're on the playground together, and he's eager to share with me this naughty secret he's just learned.

"And they also call them Tinkerbells," I say.

"Do they?!" he asks, in amazement.

"In the past, they used to."

"Do you think Tinkerbell should be mentioned in our film?" he asks, concerned.

"Tinkerbell? Sure."

He thinks about it for a moment.

"I don't think we should shy away from it," he finally says. "A faerie is what we say it is. It's a beautiful word!"

Michael goes back to slap-tapping on his leg while I reach for another candy. He breaks out in song, singing the opening refrain of the Disney film, but adding his own words: "Pixie Dust!" He slaps his hand hard against his thigh, "Hoo, hoo, hoo!"

"Disney had the story happen in one night. So the parents never even missed the kids," I say. "What do you think?" I ask him.

"Unh uh. Unh uh," he shakes his head no while unwrapping another candy.

"I sort of love that in the novel the mother has this feeling something is wrong. I can just see that. I could see her saying, 'We have to leave this party.' And then rushing home just in time to see the children flying?"

"She sees them flying?"

"Flying!" I say excitedly as I chew away at the candy in my mouth.

"At the end of the story?"

"In the first act...when Peter flies with them. When they all fly away. He's teaching them how to fly, there's a quick cut to the mother, and maybe she's holding a teacup, and she drops the teacup. You know when there's a realization something's wrong?"

I start acting out the scene.

"She drops the tea cup and says: 'We have to go!'" And the father says, "What?!" "'We have to go home!'" I say the words, casting myself in the role of the mother. "Now we cut to the flying sequence, which we build…the windows are opening like magic, and they all fly out into the night! And the parents' van comes screeching down the street, pulling into the driveway, and the parents rush out of the car just in time to see their children flying away! Just missing them, you know?!"

Michael's eyes are wide, and I keep going.

"The dog would be barking. The dog would be going crazy! Pulling at his chain, trying to break free…"

"That scene would be so beautiful!" he says, softly. Passionately. "Just beautiful! With the clouds, and the stars, and the moon."

"And when they get to Neverland it's dawn!"

"You don't suck yours," Michael suddenly announces, interrupting me.

I have no idea what he's talking about.

Now he dissolves into giggles.

"You crack yours right away!" he tells me.

And now I realize he's talking about the candy we're eating.

"Sometimes I suck them." I explain with a smile.

Who knows why, but this makes Michael laugh even harder. The double entendre for "sucking" suddenly dawns on me. And before you know it the two of us are both laughing: 3rd graders once again. We're way off track and as far from Neverland as we can possibly be. We can't even look at each other without melting into giggles. I look down at my notes and wait until the laughter subsides.

After awhile, it does.

"I like it when they leave," Michael says "And Peter says, 'You always grow up.' And he's angry... Peter's mad," he says softly. And then, he laughs. "He was mad!"

I nod.

Michael grows quiet.

"He's afraid to be alone," he tells me. "He don't want to hurt. He's trying to be tough, and he's trying to hide it. You see when the kids decide to go back, when he takes them back...," he says, explaining the last part of *Peter Pan* to me. "...he's afraid he's going to be alone again. To me he should try so desperately to get them to come back with him. You see the moonlight shining in his face, and he's talking from his heart 'cause he's afraid of being alone---He doesn't want to die."

I nod and listen as Michael explains to me about his Peter Pan.

"It hurts!" he tells me. "And that should just be really tugging at everybody," he adds, explaining how the audience will feel. "He's trying so desperately. He's tried all these generations to build up a family of people around him, and they've all left. Now this is happening again."

The way Michael is playing this last scene, explaining it to me, I can see him merging into the Peter Pan character. Peter's loneliness seems as real to me as Michael's.

"Because to me that's what *Peter Pan* is about. Not just flying to Neverland, and fighting Captain Hook," he explains. "It's very sensitive, and timid. And personal."

"I could see Wendy hugging Peter, and maybe at first he doesn't know how to hug. Maybe he's never hugged anybody before. And because Wendy is able to hug him...then I think he can hug her back at the end."

"It's got to be a big, big, big deal," he says softly.

"When Peter first appears in the play, Wendy goes to hug him, and he says, 'You can't hug me...You can't touch me...Nobody has ever touched me.'"

We sit for a moment without talking: almost reading each other's thoughts.

"And at the end he gets touched by everyone," Michael says softly.

I nod in agreement.

"These kids have gotten something very important from Peter. And in return, Peter's gotten something very important from them. It has truly been a wonderful adventure for everyone," I explain.

"Disney's releasing the animated *Peter Pan* this Christmas," he suddenly says. "Do you think that would hurt anything? What we're doing? Should we try to talk Katzenberg out of it?"

Talk him out of it?!

Katzenberg barely knows me. I only met him once at the Amblin meeting, and he called me by the wrong name. I try not to laugh at how ludicrous of an idea: a screenwriter telling the head of a studio to change the release date on a movie? Like when would that happen?

Oh, maybe never.

"Releasing it *this* December?" I ask, nonchalantly. As though this December or any December in *my* datebook makes a difference. But I'm willing to play along here. I'm crashing off the candy high, and my blood sugar is just low enough to be delusional.

"You don't think it'll hurt anything? You think it helps?" he asks, innocently. "I think it's a great idea!" I tell him, pretending I really know. "We're placing the story in modern day, so all these kids are going to already know about *Peter Pan*."

"So you're saying the cartoon will set us up?"

"I think the cartoon will set us up," I parrot back to Michael, saying it with just enough of a different inflection to make it sound original.

"Did they give you a time period when we should be done with the story?"

Nothing crashes a writer's imagination faster than a deadline.

Or the mention of one.

Reality has just peeked into our little sanctuary, this *Peter Pan* Admiration Society and Club House.

"Or are they letting us go on as long as we like?"

I've been agreeing with Michael all night. Why change now?

"Mm hm," I say, weakly.

"Good!"

I can't believe I just lied to Michael Jackson. Of course there's a deadline! Every project has deadlines attached to it, but every writer knows you don't pay attention to them. You just sign the contract, disappear, and somehow the script magically gets written, and you turn it in. Hopefully, the studio doesn't have to call and ask you for it. September seems to ring a bell. Somewhere, someone, or some part of the contract mentioned September. But I will not tell that to Michael. It's 90% about the writing, and 100% about keeping Michael happy. I want him to think he can frolic as long as he likes in Neverland. The more relaxed he is, the better the work, and the better the product. Besides, it's only March. September is a long, long way from now.

"Do you love doing what you do?" Michael suddenly asks me.

"Being a writer? Or working on this project?" I ask him.

"Being a writer."

"I love being a writer," I tell him. And I mean it—I'm glad I don't have to lie at least about that.

"…You do?" he asks me. I can't tell whether he thinks I'm kidding or not. Writers are at the bottom of the Hollywood food chain, so why would anyone just want to be a writer? As though he's thinking that very same question, Michael looks across at me, and simply asks, "Why?"

"Because I get to see the movie first," I explain. "In my imagination!"

I just hope I'm not the *only* one to see this movie.

16
Testing the Water

I had gone to Neverland, and returned safely.

Just the trip alone had helped my confidence. Being away from my house for so many hours was like running a marathon. I had made it successfully to the finish line, and the endorphins were now kicking in. Coming back from Michael's Neverland had made me feel like I could do anything.

Including writing *Peter Pan*.

My meeting with Michael in the beautiful solitude of his ranch had triggered my imagination, and my mind was rapidly filling up with ideas for the film. I bought a CD of Ralph Vaughan Williams' "The Pastoral Symphony," the music that Michael had said was perfect for Neverland, and when I played it, the sound transformed into images of Tinkerbell and the colony of faeries living underground with Michael as Peter soaring high above in the clouds.

I had found my music. I had ideas. I was ready to write.

If I could only drive to my office.

"Look at me, Mom! I'm doing it! I'm doing it all by myself!" Jacob shouts as he maneuvers his big boy bike down our driveway. His first solo flight without training wheels, he is protectively outfitted in a helmet, elbow pads, and knee-pads. If I could have bubble wrapped him, I would have done it.

David and I are standing in the driveway (with Kathryn between us) as we watch Jacob maneuver further and further away from us with each wobbly, tentative peddle. Every time he looks like he might fall, and I start to rush after him, David reaches out to stop me.

"He's going to fall!" I protest.

"He'll get back up."

Sure enough, the bike crashes, and Jacob goes with it. He ends up sitting on the sidewalk and whimpering. There are tears, I gasp, and Kathryn applauds. She likes this game her brother is playing, and she wants to go next. The only one who seems to know what he's doing is David.

"Need help?" he calls out, but never coming to Jacob's rescue. He sits there perfectly calm, after every bike crash, while holding me back forcefully from racing to my son's side with a First Aid kit, Gatorade, and boo-boo kisses. "Give him time," David quietly tells me.

And he's right.

Jacob manages to pull himself up and off the sidewalk, walking the bike a little distance to gain his confidence back, and then, he jumps on top of it again.

"I'm doing it, Mom!!! I'm doing it by myself!!!"

"My turn!!! My turn!!!" Kathryn squeals, and suddenly runs after him.

I take chase, right behind her.

Catching up, and taking Kathryn's hand in mine, I let her lead us as we hurry to Jacob's side as he peddles the bike. Running along next to him now, we head further and further down the sidewalk.

The end of the street approaches, with the busy boulevard just beyond. Braking the bike isn't part of Jacob's lesson plan yet; falling off always does the job. But this time Jacob has skillfully stayed on top, so I supply the brakes by grabbing the handlebars and stopping him just before the curb. He's not thrilled that his ride has ended.

"Mom, let me go!"

Kathryn tries to wrestle her way on top of the bike.

"Katie, no!!!" Jacob yells, emphasizing it with a push.

Kathryn falls hard, the tears come, and David runs down the sidewalk to us.

"All right, you guys, let's get home," he says, taking hold of the bike with one hand, and lifting Kathryn to her feet with the other. Jacob's wails of protest and Kathryn's sobbing fill the neighborhood.

That's when it hits me.

A rush of panic takes hold as I see just how far we've gone. We've made it all the way to the end of our block. Just one block. But to me it feels like the Gobi Desert: strange, exotic, and miles from home.

I reach out to steady myself, grabbing David's belt loop tightly.

"You okay?" he mouths, seeing my fear.

"Just keep moving," I say, giving him a feeble grin.

Across the street, I can see the thick concrete walls of the studio. Beyond them is my office: empty and waiting for me. I am so close and yet still so far away.

Obviously, walking to work is out of the question.

With unsteady legs, and my pulse racing, I hold onto David, and follow.

Jacob is back up on his bike again, this time leading us home, wobbling his way down the sidewalk. With each peddle, he rides stronger and straighter, mastering the task. His persistence and resilience is awe-inspiring.

If he can be so brave, why can't I?

"Can we take the kids to the studio tomorrow?" I ask David, as we settle in for a Saturday night of just the two of us after the kids have been put to bed. I hand him his dish of frozen yogurt, and sit close to him on the couch.

He looks at me, intrigued by the idea.

"The studio?" David knows me so well: he can tell I'm up to something. "Is this the same studio with all the scary buildings, and so many people?" he says, teasing me. "The one you don't like because it's too crowded?"

"Sunday no one is there," I explain. "It's completely empty. A big wide-open empty parking lot. Jacob can bike all over the place, and I don't have to worry about him heading off into the street."

"Like that's going to happen. He can't even stay on top of the bike," he tells me, turning his attention to the episode of *Love Boat* that's starting (our Saturday evening grown-up routine).

"We could drop off a few things at my office," I suggest.

"Really?" he asks, amazed that I'm even considering it.

"Maybe if it felt more like home it might be easier for me to go there."

David nods, liking the idea.

"If you drive us," I hesitate, the words not sure they want to come out. "I can try driving us back."

Surprised, he looks at me to see if I mean it.

I think maybe I do.

Packing up the car the next day with a bicycle, peanut butter sandwiches, boxes of juice, cookies, Baby Wipes, and sun block made it feel like a normal family outing at a park. Well, that's at least what I told myself (trying to downplay this for the sake of my nerves) as we pulled out of the driveway, and started our two-and-a-half block journey to the studio, heading into the desert like some inseparable Bedouin clan.

As soon as we pulled our car into a parking spot, Jacob and Kathryn didn't wait for us to unload the trunk before they took off running across the empty parking lot. With Kathryn squealing in excitement, Jacob raced just out of his sister's reach, jumping over every parking curb along the way, and laughing at the freedom of so much space. This was their adventure, and it was filled with a fearlessness and self-possession that I could only watch with envy.

We had a picnic lunch on the carpet of my empty office, after chasing each other up three flights of stairs. David had packed the binoculars, and the kids each took turns peering through them down at the empty studio lot below as their father read off the names of the stars painted on the parking spaces.

"'Kevin Costner,' *Dances with Wolves*, 'Sylvester Stallone,' *Rambo...*"

"Rambo?!" Jacob yells, as he reaches up for the binoculars from his dad.

"Mine! Mine!" screeches Kathryn, as she tries to yank them away.

Seeing how much fun they were having made me wonder why I ever felt so nervous about stepping out into the world. The studio seemed quiet and not threatening to me at all. At least with my family there.

Later, as Jacob peddled around the front of my building, David and I unloaded the car of all the items that could make my office feel more comfortable and more like home. Books, writing tablets, pens, a coffee maker, my CD player with CDs, a small refrigerator, and even a futon.

By the end of the afternoon, we had filled my little office with all the comforts of home. The bulletin board was now covered with hand drawn pictures that the kids had made for Mommy. Everything I could possibly need to write Michael's *Peter Pan* was sitting there waiting for me. Except for one thing: my computer.

"Uh... Don't you think you'll be needing it?" David asks, as we stand in the center of my office with the kids, and survey my new workspace. "Isn't it useful when you're writing a script?" he says, kidding me.

I was afraid to bring it.

If my computer was at the studio, but I couldn't manage to get myself there, I wouldn't be able to write at home. I had to be absolutely certain I felt comfortable enough to write there in my office before I made the ultimate commitment of moving my computer in.

Complicated thinking? Yes.

Welcome to my world.

The day was ending, but I had one more thing to do.

As David held Kathryn in his arms, and Jacob stood next to his dad at the far end of the parking lot, I sat alone in our car. I buckled myself in behind the wheel, slipped the key into the ignition, and finally (after weeks of trying), I was able to start up the car…

I release the brake, put the car in "Drive," and my foot presses down gently on the accelerator. The car moves forward, and for the first time (in a long time) I'm driving. Even with sweating palms, I am actually enjoying this as I drive around the perimeter of the parking lot all by myself. It is only a few hundred yards, but each one feels like a victory lap.

Parking the car in front of my building, I step out, and into the welcoming arms of my family.

"That was good, Mom!" Jacob says with a hug, and I help him and Kathryn into the back seat.

"How'd that feel?" David asks me, hopefully.

I grin, and nod.

"One small step." I tell him, confidently.

I toss him the car keys so he can drive us back home.

Why push my luck?

17
Hollywood Phone Games

When you're big in Hollywood, you never have to make a phone call.

Everything is filtered through secretaries, and personal assistants. Phone calls are placed for you so you never have to interrupt your day with looking up phone numbers, or talking to people you really want to duck. There are secrets to the Hollywood game of phone tag, and everyone is aware of them. Legitimate calls are placed during the workday: after 10 a.m. and before 6 p.m. When you really don't want to speak to someone, call at lunch.

"Are you available for Howard Fein?" the smoky-voiced Disney secretary asks when I pick up the phone that Monday afternoon.

Available, yes. Ready? Not really. Is a screenwriter ever ready to talk with a studio?

I look over at the Minnie Mouse clock hanging in the playroom, and it reads 1:15 p.m. I'm in luck; it's a lunchtime phone call so that probably means Howard assumes I'm at lunch, and he doesn't really want to talk to me. But if I tell his secretary I'm on my way out to lunch, then I'll owe Howard a phone call, and I really don't want to talk to him. But wait. If Howard *really* wanted to talk to me, he wouldn't be calling at lunch. So why the hell is he ducking me?

"Put him on," I say, testing the waters, knowing that if Howard really doesn't want to talk to me the secretary will come back on the line and tell me that he just stepped out or got another phone call. That's code for: he really didn't want to talk to you anyway.

Confusing? Not really. Just Hollywood.

"Good afternoon, Ms. Craviotto." Howard is on the line before the secretary has even finished putting me on hold. Not a good sign. And the fact that he's using my last name instead of my first means I might not be receiving the Disney fruit basket for Christmas this year.

"Hi, Howard!" I chirp, with my perkiest Disney female protagonist line reading.

"Darlene." Howard's voice does not sound the friendliest. "Two cars?"

"Excuse me?"

"Why does a screenwriter need two cars to go to a meeting?"

"Is this a riddle?"

I can hear him suck in the air as he struggles for control.

"Two...cars...you...took. Why does one screenwriter take *two cars* to one meeting?!"

"Is this a problem?"

"I am looking at two invoices! Business Affairs is apoplectic!" he says in the loudest of voices, just short of really yelling. This was a tone I had never heard from Howard before. I can't say he wore it well.

"I had to go all the way to Neverland," I explain. "It was so exciting! I saw Michael's bedroom. Do you know I've seen *two* of his bedrooms?!"

Howard couldn't care less.

"Drop times, turnaround times, meal penalty…" he spits out a litany of charges.

"No, that's wrong because Wayne was served lunch at Neverland, and the other driver, whose name I never got, I offered to buy a hamburger when we went through the Jack-in-the-Box in Calabassas at midnight…"

The words are spilling out of me, and I only hope I'm making sense.

Howard is not at all happy.

"Why was there a second car… no, wait, limousine?! You took a *limousine* back?!"

"That wasn't my idea. It was Michael's. Stella's really. Actually, maybe Martin is the one who called. But it was Michael's limousine, so why does Disney have to pay for it?"

"Because Michael's charging us!" he roars.

"That doesn't sound like Michael. He's very generous."

"Michael's *company* is charging us!"

"For both of the cars?"

Now *I'm* confused.

"You had a Town Car take you there."

"Yes."

"And you do know that Town Cars are cheaper…"

"Yes."

"So if you had a Town Car, why was a limo ordered?"

"Jon Peters."

"Sorry?"

"It was really Jon Peters fault. He just wouldn't leave."

"Jon…Wait…Jon Peters was there?"

"Wayne was willing to wait; he was perfectly happy to play video games until the helicopter took off with Peters, and then Michael and I met…well, first Elizabeth Taylor called…"

"Jon Peters of Sony Studios, that Jon Peters?"

"He didn't even have a car. He had this cute little red helicopter."

There was a long silence at the other end.

"Hello?" I ask. "…Howard?"

There was a loud click. And he never even said goodbye.

This is why I shouldn't answer phones when I should be writing. It was tough enough to transport my imagination into Neverland, slipping out of the characters of Peter, Wendy, the Lost Boys, and Hook, but now it was almost impossible because of the phone call from Howard.

I was sure that it must have been expensive to have two cars with two drivers, but it wasn't my fault. David was willing to drop me off at the meeting, and it wouldn't have cost Disney a dime.

I quickly make a note to tell Howard about this when he called back. Then I did a little outline of what I would say, sketching in the dialogue, and adding some stage directions about how to say it. "Parentheticals" we call them in screenwriting, and it's best not to use them a lot because directors and actors just laugh, and cross them out.

So I wasted the rest of the afternoon.

The kids came back from school, the nanny left, and when the phone rang I let the answering machine pick it up. I called later to see who it was, and sure enough, it was Howard. I made a point of calling him the next day—early. Just to avoid talking to him.

He surprises me by picking up.

"I'm coming to the next meeting," Howard announces, forcefully.

"My meeting with Michael?"

"With Michael."

"Well, no."

"Don't tell me no. I'm Disney!" he bellows.

"Michael won't meet if he knows you're coming."

"But I'm Disney!"

"It doesn't matter if you're Walt himself," I say. "Maybe if you were Bambi, you'd have a better chance."

Why was Howard pushing this? Michael and I were getting along fine, and we were coming up with ideas. Why rock the creative boat if the waters were so smooth?

"Why are you pushing this?" I ask.

"I'm not going to sit back and watch Jon Peters and Sony come courting in a little fucking red helicopter!" Howard says, angrily.

So that's what this was about: Disney was afraid of Sony stealing Michael away from them.

"Michael is excited about this project," I explain, trying to calm his fears. "He loves *Peter Pan*!"

"He loves *Pinocchio* too," Howard says, cryptically.

What's *Pinocchio* got to do with this?

I ask him.

"Sony's flirting with Coppolla for a *Pinocchio* film," he explains. "Starring Michael as Pinocchio."

Suddenly, I remembered that Michael had told me how much he loved *Pinocchio*. Maybe that's why Jon Peters stayed so long at Neverland Ranch and didn't want to leave. Peters wasn't there because of the beauty; he just wanted to make a deal. But could a Sony *Pinocchio* deal kill our Disney *Peter Pan* project?

"You need to come up with a story treatment A.S.A.P.," Howard tells me. "We need to lock up Michael before Sony comes to him with a *Pinocchio* deal."

"I can't push Michael to go any faster."

"Fine! I'll push him!" Howard exclaims. "I'm coming to the next meeting!"

"He won't meet with you, Howard."

"Have you asked him?"

I pause. My instincts are telling me it's a bad idea, but I don't know for sure. It's a moment of weakness, and Howard pounces.

"How do you know for sure, if you haven't asked him?"

"He's very skittish," I try to explain.

"But you don't know for sure unless you ask. And you owe me that!"

Howard knows me well enough to push my guilt button.

"I'm the one who hired you, Darlene. Hired you for the most sought after, hottest project in town: Spielberg & Jackson! Nobody has ever delivered those two, except for me. I got you this job, you get me into this meeting!"

He hung up on me.

I hate it when he does that.

I didn't have a choice: I had to call Stella.

"M.J.J. Productions!"

"Hi, Stella! It's Darlene!"

It was the day after Howard's "or else" phone call, and I thought it was in my best interest to touch base with my new best friend (we were on first names only) Stella.

"Oh hi, Darlene!!!!" she greets me like all of my best friends. "Michael is having so much fun working with you!"

Maybe I should get that in writing to give to Howard.

"And *thank* you for being so flexible about staying late at Neverland," she adds.

"Oh no problem!" I lie, having mastered the Art of Hollywood Conversation.

"Michael is so excited about the work you two are doing. He's anxious to set up the next meeting!"

"And uh, when do you think that will be?" I ask.

"In a month."

A month?!

"Isn't a month … rather a long time between meetings?" I ask, weakly.

"Oh no, honey. Not for Michael Jackson."

Well, maybe not on Michael Jackson's calendar. But in my Disney appointment book with the Mickey Mouse ears and the stubby hands holding my paycheck, it's way too long. Especially if we're in a race with Sony, with *Pinocchio* as their bait.

"Well, here's the thing, Stella …"

I was taking a chance. But hey, what are best friends for?

"The studio is getting a little … nervous." I tell her.

"Oh, sweetheart, they always get nervous. Just ignore them!"

I laugh. She laughs.

"No, but seriously, can you squeeze me in?" I ask desperately. "Michael and I are having so much fun! And we have this momentum going that I don't want us to lose, so can you spare a little time, any bit of time; I'll take whatever you can give me."

"You can have an hour," she says, in an official sounding

voice. Had I put too much of a demand on our friendship?
"Two weeks from tomorrow."

"Great, that'll help!" I say, reaching for my date book and
a pen.

"Got to go!" she says.

And she is gone.

No one says goodbye in Hollywood.

18
Another Side of Michael

Silence is never a good sign in a meeting.

Unless you're pausing for an effect during a pitch, when the room goes quiet, it's time for a writer to pack up and leave. I couldn't do that because Michael and I still had fifty more minutes in a one-hour meeting.

It probably wasn't a good idea to bring up Howard, and to tell Michael that a Disney executive wanted to sit in on our meetings. But I owed it to Howard to at least test the water. The water, however, was now rising dangerously, and I was definitely drowning.

We were sitting in the living room of the Hideaway; there was a noticeable chill in the air. And it had nothing to do with the air-conditioner, which was the only thing in the room making any sound at all.

When in trouble, just keep talking.

"Howard is really... he's a great... I love... I *like* Howard!" I stutter, and stammer. "I worked with him on my last Disney script, and he's very sensitive. Very intelligent. Very comfortable."

Michael's eyes become slits. He is *not* happy.

"I told him that I would check with you, but you know I was sure you wanted to keep these meetings just for you and me, and so that's what I told him, but he was just wondering if maybe for just one of these meetings, if it was okay, maybe he could just, you know, sort of, if you said all right to this, that maybe Howard could, only if you wanted it..." I ramble on, words just spilling out of my mouth. I'm afraid to stop talking.

I could feel the tension in the room, and I knew that I had caused it. I wanted to rewind the moment, and start this meeting all over again. I began to sweat, my heart started to pound, and I could feel myself slipping out of my body, hovering above the Hideaway, as I sat across from Michael, trying not to have an anxiety attack.

"Who is Howard?" Michael asks coldly, and his words bring me back to earth.

This was a new side of Michael.

Gone now was my 9 year-old playmate. The Michael sitting across from me was all business: inflexible, and controlling. It was sobering to see the difference in these two sides of his personality. I thought I had already explained who Howard was, but Michael seemed to need more information. Or maybe he was just testing me.

"Howard is an executive," I say, perceiving a slight muscle twitch in Michael's face.

It was a bad choice of words, and I knew it.

"He works for Disney," I rephrase, hoping if I used the word Disney it might suggest Mickey Mouse, Cinderella, Goofy, and all those things Michael holds dear.

But Michael wasn't buying it. He sat perfectly still, staring at me.

I tried to think of Howard's title, as though that would help.

"He's-I-think-he's-Vice-President-of-something."

Everything was just going blank in my head. I never really knew Howard's position at the studio; to me, he was just the man with whom I had story meetings. He hired me and gave me notes on my scripts. He was the door I went through to work at Disney. I never bothered to ask about his title. Not that Howard's title would even impress Michael. What was I thinking? To me a suit in Hollywood was just another suit, like an accountant really. And who brings an accountant to sit in on a story meeting about fairy dust, mermaids, and a magical island? I was suggesting that we bring a fox into the henhouse. How could I be so stupid to even ask?!

I had to get out of this. And I had to look good doing it.

"I told Howard it wasn't a good idea," I say, actually using the truth. "This is very fragile what we're doing here. We have to protect it."

I let that sit quietly for a moment. But this time the silence had meaning.

I was working it.

"Yes, we do." Michael finally says. The words were chosen carefully: I could tell he was still not certain. I had lost his trust just by introducing the conversation. He was a deer frozen in the headlights, and I could sense him stepping away from me and heading back to the forest. I couldn't chance that; I couldn't risk losing him. All the work we had been doing centered on our relationship. I knew that if I were going to work with Michael, I'd have to make sure he liked me. That he wanted to spend time with me. It wasn't enough just to be a good writer; I knew one of the reasons I'd been handpicked for this job was that Howard had convinced Steven and the studio that Michael would like working with me. Maybe it was my personal idiosyncrasies or the fact that I was a mother (and knew how to relate to children), but Howard was certain that I would be a good match for Michael on this project.

I had to prove that now.

I owed it to Howard to ask Michael if he could attend our story meetings. But more than that I had been careful not to promise. I knew that Michael would say no to having Howard at our meetings, and I had to be prepared when he did. I had to make sure that Michael understood that I was on his side, and not Howard's, proving to him that we were a creative team pitted against the insensitive, uncaring business suits of the studio.

Michael had never read any of my scripts so he had no idea how I wrote, or even if he would like my writing. Disney and Amblin had hired me, not Michael. It was important to win his confidence so that in future battles I could have him on my side. Michael needed to hear something that I had written.

"I wrote Howard a letter telling him I didn't want him to be at these meetings," I explain to Michael.

"...You wrote him a letter?" he says, intrigued.

"I wrote him a letter," I nod.

"You told him no?" Michael asks, almost looking impressed.

"I told him no," I admit. And I can see his body relax a little, the tension between us easing up.

I was taking sides, aligning myself with Michael. I was doing just what he wanted me to do.

It was 3rd grade all over again.

"Would you like me to read you the letter?"

Michael's eyes widen.

"Yes, please!" he says, with enough excitement to give me hope.

I was taking a chance here, and I knew it. The letter outlined many of the ideas Michael and I had talked about, and I wasn't sure if he would approve the sharing of those thoughts with the studio. But I had to show Howard we were working, and more importantly, I had to keep him away from these meetings. Michael needed to know that I was on his side, and no one else's. This was the only way I knew to show him that. I reached into my briefcase and pulled out a copy of the letter, and started reading it.

"Dear Howard..."

It was a long letter, and Michael didn't move at all as I read through it. I wrote Howard about our meetings, and everything we had discussed. I told him about our ideas for Neverland, and for making the film modern day. I wrote about our thoughts on the characters, and gave him the titles of the books we were using as research. And I made sure that he knew just how important Michael was in the process. The studio had been concerned about him taking the project seriously. Raymond had admitted this to me, off the record.

"They think Michael's flaky," he confided. "They know he's weird."

He had gone on to explain that it would be my job not just to write the script, but to keep Michael focused and working on the project. Of course, I didn't reference this in the letter. But I made sure that I wrote to Howard that Michael was working hard, and that it was really helping me as a screenwriter.

"...It's a joy to work with Michael," I read aloud from the letter, speaking glowingly about my collaborator who just coincidentally was listening in rapt attention across from me. "His instincts are magnificent, and I'm beginning to see Peter in him. Our time together is helping me mold the character around his unique talents. And hopefully, I'm helping him to understand the many sides of Peter."

I held my breath as I finished reading the last closing lines of praise.

Michael speaks almost immediately.

"That's beautiful!" he says, brightening for the first time all evening. "That's a beautifully written letter, Darlene!"

We are on solid ground again. The deer steps back to me.

"Can I have a copy of that? It's wonderful!" he says. "I want it for my files. We're working on a classic, and I want to document all of this."

I hope he's right.

"We're playing into that part of everyone .... The child," he tells me. "The same thing that *E.T.* did. And *The Wizard of Oz*. That's what I want to continue to have, that reality. It's fantasy, but still ... fantasy *is* reality. It becomes real ..." He goes on to explain, "How many times, and I still do ... I have dreams of flying. And for Steven to put that flight into *E.T.* was so smart! Because that's like everybody's dream, at one point or another in real life: to just take off in the air!"

"Freedom."

"Mm hm!!!" he says, passionately. "Even though it's fantasy, it's real! It's real inside of everyone! And that's what I want our film to have: all of those elements. Wow!" he can barely contain his excitement.

The letter has done its job: Michael and I are buddies again.

"You can see why I wanted to show you *Kick the Can*, right?" he asks me, connecting *The Twilight Zone* episode we watched at Neverland to *Peter Pan*. The day after returning from Michael's Ranch a messenger had delivered a VHS copy of both Steven's version and the original *Twilight Zone* episode. Michael had personally sent me the VHS tape.

"I've seen *Kick the Can* a couple of times now."

"So you've watched it?" he asks excitedly.

Once again I've demonstrated my loyalty to him.

"Since I've shown it to you at Neverland?" he says to verify my allegiance.

"Oh yeah!"

Michael smiles. I've scored big points again.

"I love the old man..." I say. And then add quickly, "In the original, I mean."

Remembering that Michael loves the original and not Steven's version.

"That old man did not want to believe that it's possible to be young again," he explains. "It became a reality, and then he believed it when he saw it. That's how Peter is, that's how he feels. He believes in all of that."

"Mm hm," I say, just to let him know I'm on his side.

"We could do such a number!" he says, excitedly. "We can get everybody going! They thought *E.T.* had emotion and truth, but something like this: the goodbyes at the end of our film, and having to choose...Do I go back and grow up, or do I stay young forever? A decision like that?! Wow!!! We could get the whole world with that! Everybody at some point has to deal with that. And just bringing it up, making it resurface again inside of everyone. We could do a number right there!"

"Growing up is the hardest thing anyone has to do," I say to Michael. "I can pinpoint when I had to grow up."

"You can?" he asks, sadly.

Growing up is not a good thing, at least to Michael. He looks at it as a loss of innocence, a dark and cynical place that lacks fun and imagination.

"My little boy came down with a high fever," I start to explain. "He seemed fine one minute, and then all of a sudden he was burning up: a 105 fever. We rushed him to Cedar Sinai Hospital, and he was only sixteen months old at the time. When a child is under the age of eighteen months, and they spike a high fever, it could be spinal meningitis. So they said: 'We need to do a spinal tap.'"

"That's serious, isn't it?" Michael asks, softly.

"They have to stick a needle in the spine to take fluid out. "

"Ohhhhhh!" Michael says, uncomfortably.

"They said to us, 'First we have to take blood from his arm, to do tests.' I have a thing about having blood drawn—When I was about four, I had to have some blood tests, and the veins in my arms were so tiny, they had trouble finding them. They were digging around in my arm with the needle, looking for a vein. And I was screaming in pain as they just kept digging. Years later, my son is sick, and they're telling me, 'We have to take blood from his arm. And you can either step out of the room, or you can stay and help us.' I thought, 'My son is so scared. He's terrified! How can I leave him?' I knew I had to stay there for him. I had to be strong."

"That's right," Michael says with a nod.

"So I had to hold him down, and comfort him as they stuck the needle in his arm."

"Ohhhhhhh!" Michael grimaces.

"And I remember thinking, 'Now I know I've grown up.'"

"Mmmmmmmmmmm."

"Jacob was crying, and calling my name, and I had to comfort him when I didn't want to be there at all. I wanted to run out of the room, break down, and just sob. But I couldn't because I was his mom. He needed me, and I had to be strong."

"Growing up was making that choice," Michael says, completely understanding.

And he's right.

Growing up is filled with hard choices: facing fear, and not running away; stepping out of the house when everything inside of you says to stay; finding the courage to drive two and half blocks; or at least to try. Somehow it was easier to be grown up and strong for my son when he needed me than to do the same for myself. All of these years I've been hiding away in my house because I couldn't be the grown up I needed me to be. I never trusted myself enough to protect me. But if I'm strong enough to take care of my son, doesn't that mean I'm grown up enough to take care of myself?

"That's a beautiful story," Michael says, breaking the silence, and bringing my thoughts back to the project. Our hour for the meeting is almost over. Someone else is scheduled to come in after me at ten o'clock. No names were mentioned by Stella, and I didn't ask. But Michael doesn't seem ready to stop talking about Peter yet.

"Do you feel we should make a certain set amount of time for these sessions? 'Cause I won't let Stella do this again," he promises.

"Next time maybe we should meet longer."

"Absolutely!" he says, enthusiastically. "And when we get to the Lost Boys I want to give them real heart and personalities, not make them The Three Stooges. Even though I love The Three Stooges, but I don't want to make them stupid, like a cartoon. You've got to care about these kids! You've got to be pulling for them. They're real! They've got feelings!" he tells me, adamantly. "Then when we reach the end it would mean so much more. We have to give them character, you know? Does Peter show favoritism to certain ones, no or yes? I'd like to see something happen at night where Peter is up and everybody is asleep…and he's by the fire…and one kid…just can't sleep, and there's a conversation between him and Peter. There's something there…about favoritism… Peter tells him something…I don't know what it is yet, but it makes the audience say, 'Now that was beautiful!' or 'That was magic!' And the boy keeps it to himself, and they decide… to…you know…" He searches for a word, a phrase, a way to express it to me.

"It's their little…," I start to suggest.

"Camaraderie," he interrupts.

"…secret." I say, finishing my thought.

The phone rings loudly, abruptly ending our conversation. It's my driver.

"I have to go!" I say, hating to leave the ball just as it was getting interesting. But the Town Car needed to get back before it turned into a pumpkin (or Disney got billed for overtime). Stella (evil woman that she was) had to be obeyed: 'Out by ten, honey. Ten o'clock sharp!' And then of course there was Michael's own life—Did the King of Pop even have a life? I wondered who was coming over at ten o'clock at night to Michael's Hideaway. I hoped it had nothing to do with work; that it was a friend. Or someone who was even more than a friend.

Michael walks me to the door to let me out.

"Don't forget my copy of that letter you wrote," he reminds me. "I want to save everything 'cause it's history. There will be books and books and books written about this. We're going to make this immortal," he says, respectfully. "Like *The Wizard of Oz* is immortal."

I smile at the thought. Could it be possible?

"This is *The Wizard of Oz* of our time!" he tells me. "This is going to be...perfect!"

I say goodbye to him, and he opens the door.

Or tries to at least. It's locked, and he seems uncertain about how to unlock it. He giggles as he twists it one-way and then the other.

"Oops!" he says with a laugh.

Finally, figuring it out, he opens it for me, while grinning proudly.

Almost, but not quite, looking all grown up.

19
No More Fun and Games

When you're a screenwriter, and you have a good meeting, you start to feel invincible. There's not a story you can't tackle; there's not a screenplay you can't write. Plot points come to you without effort, and characters are born from your wit without you ever breaking a sweat. Whatever it is that you're getting paid, it's not enough for your talents.

Or your ego.

I was beginning to feel comfortable in those studio-paid-for Town Cars that waited at my beck-and-call outside Michael Jackson's Hideaway. I liked it when the driver opened the door for me and offered me my own bottle of water in the back seat. I was beginning to feel like I deserved special treatment: I had the King of Pop's personal phone numbers (both lines directly to his bedroom), and more importantly, he loved my writing.

Well, at least my letter writing.

It was a stroke of genius (so I mused in my delusional state) to read Michael the letter I wrote to Howard, and sheer brilliance the way I was keeping one of the biggest celebrities in the world happy. It was my job, and I was (modestly speaking) nailing it. I didn't have enough hands for all the patting on my back I was doing.

That's when the phone rang rudely, crashing me back to earth.

It was dinnertime, and while one hand stirred the Cheeseburger Macaroni Hamburger Helper, the other held the phone.

"Would you *please* call Disney!" It was Raymond, sounding frantic.

This was serious: my agent was using the "P" word.

"You've been ducking their phone calls!" he yells.

"I've been working with Michael," I say, with just the right amount of pride, arrogance, and professional honor. "Disney knows this; I sent Howard a letter." I say, with a hint of annoyance. "A well-written letter," I add, with pride.

"Just *call* them." Raymond instructs before hanging up.

I could handle this. When you're certain you're the best screenwriter in the world you feel capable of handling any kind of complications thrown your way.

The studio just wanted a progress report, and I'd be happy to fill them in. After all, I had read Michael the letter I wrote to Howard (brilliantly embellished with all the ideas we had discussed), and he loved, loved, loved it. He even asked me for a copy. I would tell Disney this. Plus, we were going to meet again. Soon. All I had to do was call Stella and set it up.

Michael had told me that at our next meeting we'd have more time together. He promised that he'd insist upon it. I would happily call Disney and report all this.

But first I'd call Stella.

"Next month is looking good!" she says, hopefully.

Next month?!

"What about *this* month?" I ask.

"Already booked. But the end of next month looks possible."

Possible?!

"This month he's meeting with the President who's giving him a medal," she says, with great reverence.

And that takes a whole month?

"He's "Entertainer of the Decade" she says proudly.

"Look, Stella. We're making a lot of progress ..."

"I know, honey!" she says, interrupting me excitedly. "Michael is having so much fun! And I promised him that I would make sure to schedule the next meeting with plenty of time. No more rushed one-hour meetings. This project is just too important to Michael for that, and I want to make sure you have as much time as you need. So I'm scheduling you in for an entire evening. No interruptions, no time limits. *Next* month!"

She was good at this. And there was no way around it.

After all, he *was* meeting with the President.

"I don't care if he's meeting with God!" Howard roars, when I finally call him, and explain that Michael and I won't be meeting for another month. "Did you ask him about me sitting in the next story meeting?"

I wasn't sure how to break it to him.

"That didn't play too well, Howard."

"So he's saying no?!" he asks, incredulously.

"He liked my letter I sent you!" I say, earnestly, hoping to change the subject.

But Howard wasn't interested.

"Katzenberg is nipping at my heels!"

Howard had said the magic word: Jeffrey Katzenberg.

"He wants to know what the hell's taking so long?!"

When the head of a studio says a writer is taking too long, you *are* taking too long. No matter what your contract says. No matter if it says your deadline is September, and it's only May. May is September on Katzenberg's calendar.

"You've been meeting for almost two months," Howard tells me, sounding exasperated. "Where's the story?!!!!"

Howard was right: Where *was* my story?

I had a lot of research notes, and a briefcase filled with tapes. I'd read every book I could find on *Peter Pan*: the novel, the play, and the short story. I knew Michael wanted Hook to be evil and not to sing. He wanted Peter not to wear tights and to be friends with all the animals. He loved the Lost Boys (whatever that meant), and we needed to drop the Indians and Tiger Lilly.

But where was the story?!

Where were the plot points? The beginning, middle, and end?

I had Barrie's story, but not mine. As much as I loved spending time with Michael, giggling, and sharing our favorite moments in *Peter Pan* (*The Wizard of Oz, E.T., Sleeping Beauty,* etc., etc.), he wasn't helping me find my story.

He was getting in the way more than helping.

Like the proverbial elephant in the room, there was no way of getting around him. I couldn't just write a story without checking with Michael to make sure I was writing it the way he wanted. I had to wait weeks before I could even meet with him; and when we did meet, I wanted something from Michael that so far he hadn't given me.

Brilliance.

He was Michael Jackson, and I wanted all that and more from him. But really, who was the screenwriter here? Not Michael. It wasn't his job to be brilliant; it was mine. And all this time, I'd been looking up to him to lead the way. I wanted him to tell me what to write, and how to write it, and when he didn't, I somehow lost my way.

The truth was I had to find the story all by myself.

And I knew just where I would find it.

20
Behind the Wheel Again

There are a lot of reasons why I don't like to leave the house. Today I'm not going to let any of them keep me home.

I make that promise to myself the day I decide I'm driving alone to my office. I tell myself: Today isn't about getting somewhere; it's just about trying. Sometimes taking a first step is the biggest and most important journey of them all.

I know I will need some help, so I ask David if he can follow me there. By 8:30 in the morning, the kids are fed, dressed, hugged, and sent off to school with the nanny. Nothing stands between me and a three-minute car ride around the block.

It wasn't as easy as it sounds.

"I'll lead, and you can follow," David says as he heads for the door.

"Keep me in your rearview mirror!!!" I add quickly, as I follow after him, with car keys gripped tightly in a sweating hand.

Outside, David heads to his car, as I move with uncertainty towards the family sedan.

"Make sure you're watching me, if I need help! Just in case I get into trouble, and I need you!" I call out to him, wanting desperately to be talked out of this.

"Okay, you lead, and I'll follow," he says, opening his car door.

"Wait!" I call out to him as I hesitate outside our Taurus.

David turns to look back at me, and I take a moment to think.

"Which is better, David? Me leading or you leading?"

"What did that therapist tell you?"

I had a few years of therapy under my belt: that's why I was able to take cabs and the occasional meeting. But so far I had flunked in the driving part of the analysis. I searched in my mind for all the tips and tricks I had been taught for convincing myself that I could actually drive a car again.

"I can always pull over if I feel overwhelmed," I say, quoting the therapist.

"And?"

"I already feel overwhelmed!!!"

So much for thousands of dollars worth of therapy.

David takes a deep breath, wanting to be supportive, but not sure how.

"Well, I can see you pull over if you lead, and then I can pull over behind you. Then we'll both be pulled over before you go on again," he explains.

"Or go back," I suggest.

"You might turn back?!" he asks in exasperation. "After all of this, you'd turn back?!"

"David, no pressure!" I scold him.

I was already feeling enough pressure.

I wasn't kidding myself: the only reason I was even trying to drive at all was because I had to write Michael's *Peter Pan*. I couldn't do that at home anymore with the kids under foot. I had a deadline, a story to create, and the only place I could do that was waiting for me just a few blocks away. But the last thing I needed right now was to feel any other kind of pressure from David or anybody else. I needed to focus on one step at a time and not feel pressured to start, continue, or finish this seemingly impossible (and dangerous) voyage.

Even if it was only two and a half blocks long.

David was the one person in my life that I hoped understood this: he was my rock, and my safety net. I needed him to be strong even if I couldn't be.

"I'll be sitting in my car; you decide what you want to do," he says, and climbs into his front seat.

He was definitely losing patience, and I didn't blame him.

It was one thing to hold onto him when I was on an escalator in a department store, and filled with fear, or to cling to him while walking on a busy sidewalk, terrified by all the people. But this was a different kind of support that I was asking him to give. He had to stand off to the side now, and let me handle this.

Maybe I could do it, or maybe not.

I would just go as far as I could and find victory in that. If I went around the block, only as far as the traffic light before coming back home, that was just another step to getting where I needed to go. Tomorrow I'd try again, and the day after that, and I wouldn't stop trying until I got there.

At least I knew I was capable of sitting behind the steering wheel.

Knowing that helps me open the door of our Taurus and climb inside. Once inside, I quickly put the key into the ignition and turn it on. Sitting there listening to the idling engine, I wait for something that might push the fear away, or at least make me forget all the reasons for not driving.

I look into the rearview mirror and see Kathryn's car seat and the kids' sweaters sitting nearby. I think of how eager my kids always are to venture away from the house, how excited and fearless they are for going somewhere new and trying something different. I reach into the back seat, pick up their sweaters, and place them next to me, hoping that their excitement for new adventures might rub off a little and help me make this journey. And then, I put the car in reverse, back slowly out of the driveway and start down the street. Checking the rearview mirror, I can see David as he pulls away from the curb, and follows after me.

The first rush doesn't hit me until turning right at the corner and losing sight of my home in the mirror. Parked cars line both sides of the street, and there's nowhere to pull over. The panic only worsens. The Charlie Chaplin apartments are just to my left and seeing them somehow comforts me, reminding me of earlier times, when I first moved into the neighborhood, when driving was as easy as taking a breath, and long aimless drives took me all over the city day and night. Once upon a time, I used to do this, I remind myself.

As adrenaline washes over me, I focus on those carefree early days when anything seemed possible, especially when I was behind the wheel. Able to do anything, and not dependent on anyone for what I needed, I went wherever I wanted to go, whenever I wanted to get there. With that freedom came confidence, and I try to remember now what that felt like, hoping it can propel me (and the car) down the block.

Behind me, David follows as I drive forward, slowly making my way down the neighborhood street, heading towards the corner with its busy city traffic, and its intimidating stoplight. What will I do if the light is red? Or if it's green and goes to yellow just as I approach? Should I speed up or should I slow down? And what if I cross the intersection but David is left behind, caught by a sudden red, and too many cars to challenge it? The thoughts race through me as they always do, no time to confront them, to answer the questioning, to calm the nerves. Only enough time to trigger the fear, the panic, and the urge to flee.

I reach for the radio to turn it on: a distraction to keep me going, sounds to keep me company, to relax me, and to push away the panic as the stoplight looms ahead. Green now, but for how long? Has it just turned or is it tempting me with a false promise, soon to be yellow, daring me to make a choice: to go or to stay, or to turn around and give up. There's no time to think about it or to be sure of what to do. No planning it out, or waiting for the right answer. Just going forward has to be answer enough.

The further I go forward, the further I feel away from home. Out of sight from my house now, I'm approaching the point of no return: turning back would be just as far as going forward. My office (my sanctuary) is as close as my home is far away. The second rush hits me when I know that turning back is not an option and knowing that only makes me want to race back home even more. To pull the car over and park and to run through some neighbor's yard, scaling fences, scrambling over hedges, so desperate for safety.

Should I pull over and take a break? Collect my thoughts, turn around, and try another day? I look in the mirror and there is David, still behind me. He gives me a little wave and a crooked smile. That gets me to the corner, and by now the stoplight is red.

Oh please, God of stoplights, don't make this a long one.

Give me distractions to make me forget that I'm driving and alone behind a steering wheel. I look down and see one of Jacob's G.I. Joes poking out of Kathryn's little sweater, the one with the chocolate stain and the missing button. I am suddenly aware of the music in the car, the song playing on the radio is one that I like, and I turn it up louder.

It's Michael singing *Billie Jean*.

I smile at the irony of Michael singing to me at a time like this, as though encouraging me to keep going. To not give up.

The red light stays red for what feels like forever. I take a deep breath to keep the fear at bay, and hope I won't feel faint, or pass out at the wheel. And when I don't, when the light changes, I drive the car forward, crossing the busy Santa Monica Blvd. and I just keep going. It's too late to turn around or to give up. The office beckons me, and it's within my reach. I can't falter now; I have to keep going.

The studio takes up an entire city block, and by crossing the busy boulevard I am almost there. A quick turn right, and the car approaches the guard's booth.

Oh God, please, let my name be on the list.

Somehow I find my voice and remember my office number.

The guard actually smiles at me, and the wooden barrier lifts up.

I glance back at David, parked at the curb. He gives me a thumb's up, signaling me to go the rest of the way on my own. I turn the corner and arrive in the parking lot, still fairly empty, and offering me a parking space close to my building.

I was almost there, and that's when the third rush hit me: the thought of how far I had traveled, without a home base yet to touch. Parking the car quickly in the closest parking space to my building, I grab my workbag, slam shut the car door, and hurry to the front of the building.

It's three flights up, and one long hallway to a door with my name on it. The key is already in my hand, and the door flies open as I unlock it. My heart beating a mile a minute, I lay down on the futon near my desk. I'm out of breath, a nervous wreck, and one of my eyelids is twitching.

But I did it: I'd driven a car all by myself!

Now all I had to do was go through this again at 5'oclock.

It took me a few days to get used to driving.

For that first week, David escorted me to the studio every morning, and that first day, he was there to follow me home. By the second week, I was driving to the studio and back home again. All by myself.

Well, not exactly.

I had the company of characters that were now filling up my mind. Peter, Wendy, Tinkerbell, Hook, and the Lost Boys. All of Barrie's people were coming into my life.

Slowly, it was starting.

Writing is just like any other kind of seduction: sometimes it takes a few tricks. You put on music, make yourself a drink, fiddle with the lighting, and if you're lucky, you get lucky. Your imagination starts to work. You slip out of your own skin, shedding any cares you have in the world (including driving), and you give yourself up to another place, another time, another reality.

Once you enter it, and you're really inside, it feels as safe and secure as any place you've ever been. So safe at times, you don't want to leave it. So comfortable that nothing else exists except for you and this place where you have no needs, no problems, no responsibilities, and no restraints. All the props that helped you get there have no meaning anymore: you don't hear the music, you don't notice the lighting, you don't taste the drink, you don't see the room where you sit at a desk, in an office, at a studio.

Neverland is like this, like the warm sanctuary of an imagination waiting to be explored, available to you, and you alone. And because of its company, I am able to drive home every day. I'm never really alone because now I have Neverland with me. I bring it home every evening, and it follows me loyally when I slip behind the wheel every morning to drive to my office.

A screenwriter working on a script is never alone.

Plot points, and dialogue fill me up.

I hear all of Barrie's people now talking to one another. I eavesdrop, my pen furiously working to capture everything on the page.

By the weekend, David and I were packing up my computer and taking it over to my office: the final step away from my house.

A month went by, and I barely noticed.

Miraculously, my office phone remained quiet. Without the pressure of a deadline and the studio cracking its whip, the story rolled out of me almost effortlessly. By the time Stella called to set up my next meeting with Michael, most of the scenes had been written. If not on the page, at least there in my head. I knew where I wanted this script to go, and I was ready to write the story treatment.

All I needed next was to meet with Michael.

21
Opening Scenes and Sharing Secrets

Michael doesn't answer the door right away.

For a moment I wonder if I have the right time or the correct date or maybe the meeting's been cancelled. But when I knock again, louder, I hear him yell out, "Come on in!" When I try the door, it's already open.

"It's me, Michael!" I call to him, just to let him know.

"I'll be right there, Darlene!"

I sit on the couch, unpack my bag, and wait.

It was another 9 p.m. meeting, and I hate to admit it but I was exhausted. As much as I had looked forward to seeing Michael again, the four weeks had taken their toll. Between all the writing I was doing, the long hours at the office, and juggling the kids at night (plus the weekends), I was beginning to feel the stress.

Waking up that morning, my neck had been absolutely killing me. It was a little souvenir from that car accident I had years ago. Too much stress, not enough sleep, lots of typing, or writing longhand, and the muscles in my neck start to spasm. Whenever it happens, I put on a cervical collar and spend a few weeks living at my chiropractor's office. But with this meeting scheduled, I didn't have time to go to the doctor, and the most I could do was slip on the cervical collar. It made me nervous to be wearing it in front of Michael, but I was in a lot of pain.

You're not allowed to get sick in show business or to show any kind of physical or mental vulnerability. Television shows and films are expensive to make, and if a star, or someone "above the line" gets ill and can't work, productions might be put on hold, costing insurance companies a lot of money.

This is why Michael Jackson makes Disney nervous. All of those stories about Wacko Jacko and his eccentricities, whether true or not, give pause to those who have to write the checks and decide whether a film becomes a film. The studios and the networks care not only about our physical health but our mental health too.

That's why my agent has told me never to talk about the agoraphobia. My fear of leaving the house is not something the industry needs to know. I'm taking a big chance by wearing the cervical collar. But I feel close to Michael, and I'm only hoping that it won't make a difference to him. When he walks into the room I see right away that I'm right.

He looks like shit.

Not my words, they're his. He says them as he sits slowly in an armchair across from me.

"I look shitty," he says apologetically.

Actually, he looks exhausted. His clothes are crumpled, and his hair looks like it needs a good washing. His skin is blotchy, and on his face he wears several small band-aids. I remember that when I started this project Raymond had told me (in hushed tones) that Michael was rumored to have some kind of chronic illness.

"Lupus, I think," he had said sotto vocce. "No. Wait. Impetigo, maybe?"

He waited for me to offer what I knew, and when I refused to play this Hollywood game of star gossip, he added finally, "What's that skin condition Blacks get where their skin gets all blotchy with white patches?"

I didn't know at the time, but now I was facing it.

"I had to go to the skin doctor today," Michael admits, regretfully. "I have this condition with my skin. Sometimes it gets like this," he adds, barely audible.

I just want to hug him.

He looks drained and empty. Past exhausted. The last four weeks have been overwhelming for him, and I can see it. The traveling, the personal appearances, and the demanding schedule have all taken a toll on Michael. He's been to the White House, met the President, had meetings with Donald Trump, and accepted the Entertainer of the Decade Award. Michael's last four weeks have been filled not just with traveling and work obligations; they've also been emotionally draining.

"Ryan passed away," Michael says, softly.

Ryan White was a teenager who contracted AIDS because of a contaminated blood transfusion, and he became publicly known when his school kicked him out for having the illness. He was 13 at the time when the media learned of his story and ran with it. Eventually, he went back to school (through a long legal battle), and he became a kind of celebrity. Michael befriended the boy, and Ryan, with his family, spent the last Christmas at Michael's Neverland Ranch.

"He got really sick," Michael adds. "And they put him in the hospital." He shakes his head sadly. "But he didn't make it."

I can see the beginning of tears as they start to form in his eyes.

Ryan died on April 8th, three days after Michael had received a special National Accommodation from President Bush on the front steps of the White House. The funeral was a few days later, and Michael was there in attendance. It's been a rough couple of months. In February, Malcolm Forbes died, and Elizabeth was beyond consoling. In March, Michael had performed for the Sammy Davis Jr. Tribute; the singer had throat cancer and was dying. Recently, Elizabeth Taylor was hospitalized and battling the complications of pneumonia. And in the last few days, Michael's own grandmother has passed away.

"I feel like I'm surrounded by death and illness," Michael says, softly.

"We don't have to do this," I tell him. "We can meet some other time."

"No, I love this!" he says, showing a little more energy. "This'll make me feel better. Please, I want to do it."

"Okay, but we can stop whenever you want."

He nods and grows silent.

"I look so shitty," he says once again, embarrassed by it.

"Well, I feel shitty," I confess.

Michael laughs weakly and so do I. Suddenly, he notices the cervical collar.

"What happened?" he asks with great concern.

I picked the wrong night to wear a cervical collar. I'm another person in Michael's life with some kind of illness. I downplay it quickly.

"I just wear this when my neck gets tired." I explain, trying to sound so very healthy. "No big deal," I say, mustering a big smile as I undo the Velcro patch in the back of the cervical collar. Removing it, I stash it away in my workbag, while making a mental note to book my chiropractor for all of next week.

The room is suddenly filled with silence.

This is a crucial meeting to the project, and I need Michael's input. I don't want to start writing the story treatment if he doesn't like the plot points I've created and all of my scene ideas.

But Michael looks preoccupied, and I wonder if he can even work tonight. It's hard to be creative when your personal life is in turmoil. If you're not a celebrity, you can take some time off, a few days, a week. When I was my most phobic and couldn't get out of the house, I told my agent not to book me any work for a few months. I stayed home and wrote a spec script while secretly I learned how to feel comfortable enough to take cabs so I could eventually go to meetings. But when you're Michael Jackson, people expect you to just keep working. No matter how hard you hurt, or how shitty you think you look. You're paid to pull it together, and that's what Michael has to do now.

I try to help him by taking the lead.

"I've been working on our story," I say. "Putting it together scene by scene. I'm starting to see the film in my mind."

Michael looks at me, just waiting to be led. He's not able to give anything more than just showing up. It's up to me to be the leader, to put my ideas on the line. And maybe to put my job there too.

"I want to read you something," I say, as I reach for my workbag. I'm taking a risk here I know it. If Michael doesn't like what I've come up with, I won't have a story treatment to give Disney. "Would you like to hear the opening of the film?" I ask, pushing past the panic that is slowly building inside of me.

"The opening?" he asks in surprise.

"I wrote it yesterday," I tell him. "Would you like to hear it?"

"Yes, please!" he says, excitedly.

Reaching into my workbag, I pull out the pages. I take a long sip from my glass of water and try to quiet the nerves inside. I focus on the words in front of me, trying to forget where I am and who is listening. I try to remember what it feels like to read a story to my children at night: to put myself in what is written, to fly away there in my mind, to become the story, and the people in it.

Slowly, I begin to read:

"It is a night like no other night. The sky is filled with clouds highlighted by a hidden full moon. They are the softest, and largest clouds we have ever seen. There are no stars in the sky—except for one. Its brilliance catches our attention. Is it our imagination, or does it seem to be growing brighter, moving closer to us? Heading downwards, leaving the sky—it streaks towards the earth, bearing towards a small lake that's nestled within a forest.

A heavy mist hangs low over the water. The night grows suddenly still. All sounds stop. The crickets and the night animals are quiet: waiting and watching. Streaking downwards, the falling star cuts through the mist like a bright beam of light, like a laser skimming across the water. And as it touches the land, the air explodes into a million twinkling lights—like the sparks from a child's sparkler. In the middle of the radiant lights we see a dark figure standing on the shore. Faceless, but with the features of a young man, it is a three-dimensional shadow.

The shadow looks around—surprised by its sudden freedom. We hear a whistle—crisp, and distinctive, like a young boy's searching for his dog. The shadow hears it too, and takes off running, skittish like a deer in the woods.

The mist upon the water slowly begins to part, and walking out of it we see a young man. His face is hidden in darkness; above him, hovering over his head, is a single red twinkling light. As the young man steps upon the shore, this twinkling bright companion streaks in front of him, changing colors from red to blue, and settling on top of his shoulder, illuminating his face. And this is how we first see Peter Pan: by the bright and twinkling light of Tinkerbell.

Peter looks around, searching for his shadow. The shadow hides behind a tree, playing a game with Peter of 'Hide and Seek.' Peter, like a child, plays along, chasing after his shadow in full pursuit. Catching up with it in one moment, and then losing it again. It becomes like a dance—as Peter and his shadow move gracefully through the forest.

The shadow races out from the trees into a clearing at the top of a hillside. With a great leap, the shadow jumps from the hillside as Peter chases after him, with Tinkerbell at his side. They stop suddenly when they reach the clearing at the top of the hill, and looking down below they see a residential street on the edge of a city.

Peter looks intrigued by this sign of people—the closeness of the real world within his grasp. He's cautious and not sure he should follow. But his shadow beckons to him on the street below. And like a boy in the middle of play, Peter cannot resist. Tinkerbell stays close to his side as Peter leaps from the hillside.

Peter chases his shadow through the dark and empty early morning streets. And then, up onto the rooftops, the game of tag at its peak. Peter and his shadow are too noisy, and a dog barks. Peter quiets down. Whispers. Snaps his fingers. And tries his special whistle once again. Finally, his shadow joins up with him, and just at the moment when we are sure that they have re-united, the shadow in one final burst of freedom, flies away—diving head-first through an upstairs open window of one of the houses."

I stop reading. It's all that I've written.

"That is so beautiful!" Michael whispers dramatically.

I smile, relieved that he's happy.

"I want to hear more!" he says excitedly.

"It's not written yet!" I laugh.

"Oh Darlene, that's wonderful. It's wonderful!"

"Can you see it?" I ask him, hoping he was able to visualize what I wrote. "Can you picture it onscreen?"

"All of it! I can see all of it! The shadow, and Peter chasing it. And Tinkerbell's light changing colors as they run. That's so beautiful!"

"It just came pouring out of me. The other day I saw it in my head, and I wrote it down as fast as I could!"

"Is that how you work?"

"When it all comes together, I just close my eyes, and see it."

"Mm hmm! Me too!"

"It doesn't even feel like I'm writing it," I explain. "It's just like I'm watching this movie, and writing down everything I see in my mind."

"Mmmmm…That's the way I work," Michael says with a smile.

"Sometimes it pours out so fast it's hard to get it on paper."

"When it comes out, I think, 'Where did that come from?'"

"That's how it works," I nod in agreement.

"It's fun to create!" he says with a laugh. "When you feel unbounded, there are no limitations. Let your mind soar!"

"I read this to my kids last night."

"You did?" he asks.

"They loved it!"

"It's good, Darlene. You *know* it's good!" He giggles, like a kid sharing a naughty secret. "If the rest of the screenplay is as good as this, the film will be incredible!"

"I hope so—My kids really loved it."

"Kids know what they like. That's why I love children! I love them!" he adds passionately. "I used to go to the hospitals, and I still do when I can, where they deliver the babies… and there's this room, just babies everywhere. And I go in there, and I feel so gooood! And I start to giggle, and laugh…" He giggles quietly as he remembers. "…and you hear them making these little baby noises, these little sounds. And I get to hold them, and grab them. It's such a great feeling! It's excellent! And so pure! Mm hmm!" he nods, certain of what he's saying. "And how old is your baby?

"Two. I have two."

"You have *two* children."

Before you know it, I've got their photos out from my purse, and I'm showing them to Michael.

"Jacob and Kathryn…Katie," I say, proudly.

"Jacob and Katie," Michael repeats their names, trying out the sound, and smiling. "I like that name for a girl—Katie."

I hand him a photo of Jacob with his arm proudly around his little sister.

"Now, that's sweet!"

"Kathryn calls you 'Apple Jacks' because she can't say your name."

Michael laughs.

"Apple Jacks!" he repeats, liking that. He looks over at me, conspiratorially, "Now, I know it's hard to admit it…But do you have a favorite? Between you and me."

No one has ever asked me this before. I'm not sure how to answer. What do I tell him? What does it matter? He's Michael Jackson, who's he going to tell? The *Star*? I could easily confess anything to Michael, and it would never get back to anyone in my life. Michael lives in a protective bubble, hidden safely away in his own private Neverland. The more I've gotten to know him, the more I understand this. It's the one thing we truly share in common. I've been isolated in my own private bubble too, tucked safely away in my house.

"Depending on which one of my kids is the nicest to me at the time, that's the one I like the best," I confess, with a grin.

He laughs at that, and so do I.

Michael looks at a second photo, one of Kathryn dressed as Snow White standing next to a makeshift playhouse fashioned out of a large cardboard shipping box.

"Isn't that sweet!" he says, looking closer. "And what's that? A box?"

"It's a little castle we made out of a couple of cardboard boxes that we painted pink, and we put Cinderella stickers all over."

"Mmmmmm," he says, intrigued. As he studies the sagging, homemade playhouse that Kathryn stands next to with great pride, Michael stares long and hard at the picture, as though trying to understand it. I guess no one ever made anything out of an old box for him when he was a kid. Not that he was a kid for very long. Performing at eight and earning a living sounds to me a lot like being a grown-up.

Whether Michael admits to it or not.

Over the next few hours I share with Michael all of my story ideas. I tell him about Hook's evil ways and Peter's innocence. I sketch in the faeries that live underground, underneath the hollow hills of Neverland. I tell him about the faerie dust that makes mere mortals fly. How Hook wants to find it—the ultimate treasure—to be able to fly and to go back into the world for his own evil ways. When I tell him that Hook's presence is so evil that it's the reason the Lost Boys are growing older and leaving Neverland, he delights in this part of the story.

"That's great, Darlene!" he says. "Not only is he threatening the land, he's threatening everybody in it."

I tell Michael all about Peter, and his innocence, how he's modeled himself after the faeries because he's grown up with them. Peter doesn't cry because faeries don't cry: They just change the subject.

"Mmm Hmmm!" Michael says, loving the idea.

"The first time Peter cries is when Tinkerbell dies."

"Mmmmmmmm!"

"Hook is responsible for killing her. And when she dies….Peter takes her to this hillside where there's this single tree. He puts her down, and covers her with petals of flowers. There's a close up of Peter's face and a single tear runs down his cheek. And that's because he's *human*! He's not like the faeries. And this is the first time he's really cried. He can cry now because when Tinkerbell dies, the magical powers Peter has, which he's gotten through Tinkerbell, those powers die too. It means he can't fly anymore. So now when Peter goes and meets with Hook, and they have that big battle, he has to face Hook man-to-man."

"Peter fights him!" Michael says with pleasure. "Unreal, unreal!!!"

"Everybody's going to be pulling for Peter because he's just lost his best friend, and now he has to fight Hook, and we'll be thinking, 'How is he going to win? He's not as strong as Hook!' He's a pure, wonderful guy and he's got to go up against this real tough, mean, sonofobitch. And how is Peter strong enough to fight Hook? But it's because of Peter's wonderful spirit, and purity of heart that will enable him to win.

It's good versus evil, and good wins out at the end. Hook is defeated! And when that happens, Tinkerbell comes back to life, and the faeries rise up from underground to take back Neverland again."

I push the story forward, explaining, and hoping that he understands. And as I do, I see Michael become Peter Pan. So vivid is the image in my mind I can't recall knowing Peter as anyone else. That magic that happens when a character fleshes out into an actor, body and soul, happens this night twenty-four floors high above Wilshire Blvd.

For me, Michael becomes Peter Pan forever.

If I was worried about Michael's energy, I was wrong. We've been talking for hours, and he's showing no sign of slowing down. I only hope I have enough tapes to last through this meeting.

"Are we going to care about the Lost Boys?" he asks, sipping at his water.

I laugh, and he looks over at me, puzzled. He doesn't understand why I seem to be laughing at him.

"You've asked me that … !"

"Have I asked you that before?!" he asks in total surprise.

"Like a thousand times!" I say, incredulously.

"I'm sorry, Darlene," he says in the most contrite, and innocent of voices.

I feel like a bully. The room fills with silence, and I can sense Michael retreating. Was it my tone of voice? The fact I laughed at him? Definitely, all of the above. He is slinking back deeper into his armchair, growing quiet, and unreachable.

"That's okay, Michael…That's all right," I assure him, trying to coax him back. "We've got to love the Lost Boys," I assure him.

"We've got to love them," he says in agreement.

"Because in the end…"

"I didn't know I asked you that before," he interrupts, laughing.

"Oh that's okay."

"That just concerns me so much," he says, earnestly. "These are kids who are trying to survive," he says strongly. "They're very loving, and they're trying to help each other to make it. If you make them stupid, you don't care about them."

"Peter is like their father, and their mother rolled into one," I explain. "He's really taken care of them. And in the end the Lost Boys go back with Wendy, Michael, and John. That's a big thing for Peter; he has to say goodbye to these boys. So we've got to love them because then we'll say, 'Oh no! Peter is going to be all alone!' And at a certain point Wendy says, 'Peter…Come with us.' Can you imagine the conflict going on within Peter?"

Michael reaches over to the tape recorder, and shuts it off.

"And you think Steven will go for all of this?" he asks me.

The sound of his name stops me cold. Like the ticking clock inside of the crocodile that terrifies Hook, the mere mention of Steven frightens me just as much. It carries the same threat: I risk losing everything. All of the work I've done, painstakingly building *Peter Pan* around Michael, means nothing if Steven doesn't like it. I can only hope he does. For Michael's sake, I better sound stronger and more certain than I feel at the moment.

"We just have to be strong," I tell him. "We have to be together on this,"

"We have to make sure he does this the way we want it," he says. There is no sign of the boyishness or innocence Michael usually shows. Clearly, he will not be backing down from the kind of *Peter Pan* that he wants to make. If any compromises will be made, Steven will be the one to make them.

"The same actor can't play Hook, and also the father," I reiterate the point Michael has always made. "It's just wrong because Hook is the villain. You can't have the father as the villain."

"I hated my father," Michael suddenly says quietly. Staring off, he becomes lost in his own thoughts. "Growing up, I hated him."

I'm surprised by the revelation. Embarrassed by it too.

"... Really?" I ask softly.

"Oh yeah ... He was mean. He'd hit us."

I don't know what I should say, or if I should say anything. I just listen.

"I hated him. I really did!"

The room grows silent. I wait for a long time.

"But that doesn't work for this story," Michael says, knowing that the story has to take precedence over whatever feelings he has about his own father. "To have the father as the villain doesn't work." He looks over at me. "Don't you agree?"

I nod. I agree.

Michael reaches over and turns the tape recorder back on and sips at his glass of water.

"The parents shouldn't be there for the children though," Michael says. "They should be too busy to be around them."

"Yes, you're right. But they can't be cruel parents.

"They're just too busy," Michael explains. "And the kids… they love their parents even the ones that are never there for them, or who don't spend any time with them. They love them, these kids…even to the point of coming home to an empty house after school. Fixing their own afternoon meal, and watching TV. But there's that emptiness inside of them. All the kids I know…I have to be honest…I don't think their parents give them enough love, enough compassion, or give them the time they need. And somebody else sails that course for them. Kids will find parenthood in another individual if you're not there for them. And with my father, he was never there. So I'd find people that I liked being with, and they would become my father. It's so easy to understand why Peter would take them away because they're not totally happy kids."

"That's the sadness—it's from not spending time with their parents."

"I wish I could take them all and love them," Michael says, in the smallest of voices.

Suddenly, the room grows silent. Michael sits so quiet and still. I look at my watch: it's almost midnight. I miss my kids. I want to go home.

"We can knock off anytime," I suggest to Michael.

"Huh?" he answers, looking tired and a little bit lost.

"We can stop now," I tell him, softly.

He reaches over to the end table and picks up his fedora hat that's been sitting there for the entire meeting. Now, he plops it on top of his head.

"I should be wearing this," he says, softly.

"Why?"

"I haven't washed my hair," he explains, embarrassed by it.

I start to pack up my workbag and reach over for the tape recorder.

Michael pulls the brim of his hat down low over his head, and slumps back into the cushions of the armchair. He looks beat.

"I'll give you copies of these tapes, so that you can have them too." I tell him.

He brightens at that idea.

"Oh great!" he smiles. "Excellent!"

I stash the recorder and its tapes back into my leather bag.

We've spent the whole evening discussing the story, and the only step left now is for me to start writing. I need to go on to the next stage. I want Michael to understand this. Not to get his permission, only to let him know.

"I'm going to start writing up the story, scene by scene."

"Great!" he says, momentarily brightening.

I hesitate a moment. Not sure I should bring it up, but knowing that I must.

"At some point, we'll have to talk to Steven," I say.

He looks over at me; his jaw tightens.

"We need to share this story with him so he understands the direction we're taking it," I explain. "I'll put in everything that we've talked about, all of our ideas from the opening to the ending."

"I want to hear it first. *Before* Steven," he says in a tone of voice that can't be challenged.

This is the side of Michael I fear the most.

It shuts me out. And every laugh we've shared, every moment of connection we've had between us, feels insignificant. It's as though we've never even connected at all.

"After I type it up, I'll come here and I'll read it to you if you want."

"I'd like that," he says, his voice no longer cold or so commanding. He's back to being Michael, so polite, so filled with wonderment, mischief, and innocence.

"Next time we meet!" I promise him.

"It's going to be great!" Michael says, excitedly. "From everything you've read to me, if you can put it down on paper like this, it'll be beautiful!"

"We might have to fight with Steven to make him see things the way we've talked about them. To let him know this is what we want to do," I explain.

"We have to make him listen," Michael nods in complete agreement. This time he says it like a collaborator and not the superstar demanding it be done his way.

Maybe because it's late, or because we're both tired, I hesitate before leaving, wanting to share one more thought before I go.

"It's strange... I had a dream the other night," I tell him. I hadn't planned on sharing this with him, but for some reason I want him to know. It was a vivid dream, one that I've had trouble shaking. "It was about Steven," I tell him.

"It was?" he asks, surprised.

"He was sick, really sick, and he was in the hospital. I went to see him. I was a doctor, and... actually, I was there to help him. When I asked them at the hospital what Steven's problem was, you know what they told me?"

"What?"

"His heart."

Michael's eyes widen.

"I was a cardiologist in the dream."

"That's beautiful...!" he tells me. "You were there to fix Steven's heart," he says slowly and with a big smile.

"It feels funny saying something like that..."

"Why?" he asks. "Steven does need help with his heart. He really does."

"It just sounds so narcissistic saying I'm the one to fix it."

"Everyone has special gifts," he tells me. "The way you write…that's your gift to the world—that heart you put into your words. We all have gifts, Darlene. Mine is to bring beauty into the world," he says, simply. "I'm like one of the Apostles…It's up to me to present the Word of God."

He says this modestly, as though this statement is just a part of life. Not proud or boastful, he seems to accept this sanctified role as a fact of nature, like the sun's warmth or a rainbow after a storm.

I'm a little surprised that he's shared this with me. I don't think he would have admitted his holy calling if I hadn't confessed my own egocentric dream about saving Steven. It's after midnight, and we are both sharing secrets that perhaps we might not be comfortable sharing in the daylight or with anyone else.

"That's why this film is going to be great," Michael says, with a smile, and a real sense of conviction. "Our *Peter Pan* will be perfect!"

Talk about feeling pressure.

22
Unexpected Guests

The next few weeks were hell.

I locked myself in my office, turned off the telephone, and started to write up the story treatment. Or at least I tried to write it. I didn't like anything that was coming out of my computer. I tried doodling, sketching out the characters, hoping somehow to entice them out of my imagination and onto the page by visualizing them. But it was no use: Peter, Hook, and Tinkerbell had deserted me. Even listening to Ralph Vaughan Williams didn't help. It only made me fall asleep and dream I was flying until I crash-landed and woke up in a sweat.

I felt like I was betraying J.M. Barrie. I was "Spielberging" everything for the big screen by taking this quirky little story and blowing it up in size with special effects and million dollar sets. *Peter Pan* is a classic, but I was about to rip it open, tear it apart, and piss on it like some dog claiming my own territory. I was creatively paralyzed by having to be Steven's cardiologist, while performing the holy task of presenting Michael's Word of God. I couldn't write a thing. I was too busy trying to be brilliant.

Every writer writes with an audience in mind. The problem was that I was writing for Michael Jackson, Steven
Spielberg, and Team Disney. I had forgotten my real audience: children. Barrie wrote *Peter Pan* for those four little
boys he befriended in Kensington Park, London. Those kids
were Barrie's audience, and he never lost sight of that, telling
them bits and pieces of his story each day as he wrote it. I had
my own audience at home: my two kids who loved *Peter Pan*.
So why wasn't I writing for them? Once I remembered this,
the words started to flow.

Each night I would read to Jacob and Kathryn the pages of
the *Peter Pan* story that I had written that day in my office. The
children would listen at bedtime as I acted out all of the roles,
moving the story along with my voice. When they'd laugh, I'd
remember the sound, and it gave me hope; when their eyes
grew big, and they listened so spellbound, I knew that my story was working.

I finished the treatment and called MJJ Productions to set
up a meeting. I had made Michael a promise that he would
be the first to hear the story, and I wasn't about to break that
promise.

"Michael will be thrilled!" Stella says happily when I call
her to let her know the treatment is done. "I'll get back to you
with a date," she promises, and when she calls later that day, I
take it as a good sign that the meeting will happen right away.

"Next Thursday at 9:30 p.m." she tells me.

I was ready.

My Town Car pulls into the circular driveway in front of Michael's building right on time. We park behind a pizza delivery truck, and I grab my workbag as I climb out of the car.

The doorman is paying a delivery boy for a large pizza.

"Dinner?" I ask him, with a wink.

"Yeah, I wish!" he says, taking the pizza box in hand. "Actually, this is going up to Michael's."

I smile. How nice! Michael must have ordered a pizza for our meeting. Maybe he's been working all day, or maybe he thinks I might get hungry from reading the treatment to him. Very thoughtful, I tell myself. Hope there's no bell peppers; I hate bell peppers on pizza.

"There's an old guy up there with him," the doorman tells me.

"Excuse me?" I say.

An old guy?

He was a young doorman, so old to him might mean anybody over 40. Could he mean Steven? Michael never said anything to me about having Steven at this meeting. Stella didn't mention it when she called me back to give me the date and time. And besides, I wouldn't call Steven old.

"An old guy?" I ask the doorman, thinking maybe I didn't hear him correctly.

"Well, he looks old. He's got white hair, and a white beard."

Sounds more like Santa Claus than Steven Spielberg.

"He's got a kid with him," the doorman explains, like that should suddenly make sense to me.

It doesn't.

"Maybe I screwed up and got the wrong date," I suggest.

"Let me call up and see," he says, and reaches for the house phone. Someone answers right away in Michael's penthouse, and the doorman tells him that I'm downstairs, ready for my meeting. After a moment, he looks over at me and smiles, giving me a thumbs-up.

The meeting is definitely on.

It's a fast elevator ride up to the penthouse, not nearly enough time to figure out what exactly is going on. This meeting tonight is so I can read the story treatment to Michael and Michael alone. Now it feels like I'll be walking into a pizza party.

Who exactly is the old man? And why is there a kid at Michael's at 9:30 at night? I'm thinking they must be houseguests; maybe there's an extra bedroom I don't know about. Or connecting doors that lead to another penthouse. I'm hoping that when Michael answers the door he'll explain everything. "I'm running late," he'll say. "This is my uncle," he'll tell me, introducing the old man. "And my niece," he'll add. "They're leaving right now, but we're having a quick slice before they go. Help yourself, there's no bell peppers!"

That would make sense. I would buy that.

But Michael isn't the one who greets me at the door. The man who welcomes me is large and portly looking. He does indeed have white hair and several days' growth of white whiskers. But he's not Santa Claus, and I doubt he is Michael's uncle.

"You must be Darlene," he says with a smile. "I'm Buddy!"

Okay, so that name means nothing to me. I don't know him; Michael's never spoken about him, and I haven't even a clue what he's doing there. I must look confused because Buddy goes on to explain, "Michael asked me to sit in on this meeting."

Ok...Wait. Why?

Of course I don't ask him that, or say anything really; I just step inside the penthouse as though everything is fine, everything is status quo. I smile and finally find my voice, "Nice to meet you, Buddy." Not really. But what's a screenwriter to do? He's Buddy, and he's here, and I just have to deal with it. Stay loose and keep smiling. I can do this, I tell myself as Buddy escorts me into the living room. I can adjust to this.

Or maybe not.

We are in the living room now, and what I see confuses me even more. Michael sits on the couch wearing his black fedora, and sitting at his side is a little boy also wearing a black fedora. The boy is polishing off the pizza slices as Michael giggles and pours him more soda. The child looks like he might be nine or ten years old, and Michael appears as comfortable sitting next to him as I've ever seen him look.

"Hi, Darlene!" Michael says, never moving from the couch.

I'm sure my mouth must be open. I only hope it's not.

"This is my friend Andrew," he tells me, as though that makes everything else understandable.

I nod and smile at the little boy who is too busy wolfing down pizza to really care who I am or why I'm there. I really don't know what to say. For someone who makes her living using words, those tools of my trade are suddenly not at my disposal. I am trying not to stare, but I don't understand this strange image of dual fedoras or the significance of Michael and his pintsize pizza buddy.

"Andrew's from New Zealand," Michael says, as though that will explain this strange tableau.

I'm still not getting it.

Except I remember back to the night of the Grammys when Michael told me that he had children all over the world. He pointed to that special phone on the nightstand next to his bed, and he had said to me that children were the only ones that had his special phone number. "I have kids all over the world," he had told me proudly. Maybe this boy is one of those kids. But it's difficult to figure out who he is or what is going on because this scene is not exactly what I planned in my head for tonight's meeting.

Buddy is smart enough to see that I look lost.

"Andrew's mother is a friend of Michael's," he explains, with just the right amount of offhandedness. "They're visiting from New Zealand."

New Zealand. Guess that answers everything.

I take a seat and join the party. What else can I do?

"I'm going to read the treatment to you tonight," I tell Michael.

"Yes, I know!" he says excitedly.

I look up at Buddy and over at little Andrew. This is the part of the scene when Michael is supposed to say, "They'll be leaving after Andrew finishes his pizza." I take a little beat and wait for Michael to say his lines. I look over at him, and he just smiles.

"I can't wait!" he says, giggling.

That's when I realize they aren't leaving. Not old man Buddy, who was asked to sit in during this meeting, and certainly not little Andrew the boy from New Zealand. Neither one of them is going anywhere. All eyes are on me, the main headliner of the evening. I guess I'm the dinner show.

"I didn't know I was going to have an audience," I say, pointedly, but as tactfully as I can manage. "I thought it was going to be just you and me," I look over at Michael, hoping for some explanation.

"Didn't Stella tell you?" Michael asks with wide eyes and total innocence.

"Stella did *not* tell me," I say, attempting to cover my confusion and frustration with a little grin.

Michael puts his hand up to his mouth, coquettishly.

"Whoops," he says.

Whoops, indeed.

Buddy can sense my professional reluctance.

"I've worked with Michael before," he explains, as though that makes everything all right.

It doesn't.

"Buddy is a producer, and writer," Michael tells me.

Okay, now I'm panicking, and the last thing I need right now is a full blown panic attack. I take a breath, and try to relax. I try to distance myself from what is happening here in the room.

What the hell *is* happening in this room?!

Why is another writer here? The last thing a screenwriter on a project needs to hear right before pitching her story to the star is that there is another writer (not even attached to the project) sitting in the room. Is this some kind of test Michael is putting me through? If I fail it am I going to be replaced? Was it something I said at the last meeting? I know I pushed hard to keep Michael focused: Did I push him too hard? I laughed at him and pointed out that he kept repeating how much he wanted the Lost Boys to be real and likeable. Maybe I hurt his feelings. Did I violate some undefined etiquette between star and screenwriter? The problem with the film industry is that nobody tells you the rules; you only learn them after you break them.

Buddy must be a mind reader.

"I mostly produce," he explains, recognizing the look of competitive horror in my screenwriting eyes. "And I've done a couple of songs with Michael," he adds.

"Buddy and I just wrote a song together," Michael clarifies. "I want him to hear the story to get some ideas for songs."

I look at Buddy for confirmation, and he smiles.

I'm not sure I totally trust him. But for the moment, I have no choice. I have to somehow push through this awkwardness and fear to read my story, and I can't be worried that I'm auditioning for a role I already have. I have no choice but to suck it up and go through this.

"Terrific!" I say, lying with great enthusiasm. Reaching inside my workbag, I pull out my little tape recorder that's been present at all of our meetings, and I set it on top of the table in front of me. I sense Buddy watching me closely, so I hesitate before pushing the red record button.

"I always tape these meetings. Michael likes me to tape them, and it's something I usually do at all of my story meetings," I explain to Buddy. "Do you mind?"

Buddy gives me that well polished Hollywood smile again. "Actually, I do."

Oh shit.

I look over at Michael, waiting for him to speak up, hoping he'll say something. He's wanted all of these meetings to be taped, so why isn't he insisting we tape this meeting too? Unfortunately, his attention is on the boy as they discuss the merits of pepperoni versus double cheese. Michael seems content to have Buddy run this meeting while he centers his attention on the little boy. If I was hoping for Michael to back me up, I am out of luck. Reluctantly, I place the tape recorder back into my bag and mentally kick myself for even asking permission to use it.

Andrew by now has finished the pizza and flops back into the couch cushions. Michael cleans up the pizza box and used napkins, taking the trash into the kitchen. Buddy and I wait for Michael to return, and my eyes look over at the freckled-faced little boy whose mop of blonde hair peeks out helter-skelter under the brim of the fedora.

What the hell is he doing here?

And where is his mother? It's ten o'clock on a Thursday night, and shouldn't she be here? My head is spinning with questions that I can't possibly ask. Instead, I reach for the glass of water Buddy has poured for me from the glass pitcher Michael always seems to have available.

Michael returns with a blanket, and settles back down on the couch, covering the boy and himself with it. He puts a protective arm around little Andrew, and the boy settles back into the crook of Michael's shoulder. I try not to stare. I try not to watch this or to look judgmentally as Michael spreads the blanket over his lap, and the lap of the little boy, the two of them cuddling closely together.

I put my head down, and look at the pages of my story in front of me. Once I am certain that everyone is settled down (and tucked in), I begin to read.

Helen Hayes once said that actors have to be able to slip in and out of their bodies at will to sometimes watch the play with the audience or to observe the audience itself. You learn as an actor how to slip out of the reality of the play, and into the reality of the actor watching the play. I was stage trained as an actor, and this out of body experience is something that has stayed with me. Sometimes it can be frightening, however, to slip out of your body and to watch life while hovering above from a distance.

But that's what I was doing.

As I read through the 37 pages of my *Peter Pan* story, I moved from Neverland, to Michael's Hideaway, watching everything in the room while living the story on the page. No one would know I was doing it, but I was. I read the lines of dialogue in character; I would play a dramatic moment, and then I'd quickly hover just above myself, turning my attention to Buddy or Michael or the drowsy looking little boy cuddling with Michael.

I'd take flight as Peter, soaring above treetops, but I'd also watch Michael and the little boy sitting across from me. As my mind focused on the beauty of Neverland, it also struggled to make sense of what was happening in this Westwood penthouse. As I lowered my voice and slipped into Hook, I hovered above Michael, watching him cuddle with the boy the way that I did with my own children. But this wasn't Michael's child, and he wasn't the boy's mother. He didn't seem to relate to this boy the way I've seen fathers relate. His moves were like those of a mother: comforting and tender as he would reach out and take the little boy's hand to hold it.

I've never thought of Michael in terms of gender, but seeing him here on the couch with this boy makes me think more of a woman than a man. I don't know what that means, or what to do with these thoughts that I'm having. I only know that my instincts are telling me this doesn't feel right.

It just doesn't.

The little boy falls asleep at the end of the big cave scene where a wall painting made by the now extinct Indians becomes animated, and we see the history of Neverland, learning about the treasure of the fairy dust. I'm of course hovering over the room as I read this scene, so I notice the boy's closed eyes before anyone else does. It's the end of Act Two in a three-act structure, and it's a good place to stop reading.

I look up from my story.

"I think he's asleep," I say to Michael with a stage whisper.

Tenderly, Michael bundles the little boy in his arms and lifts him up from the couch. He carries him off carefully towards the hallway and to his bedroom.

My eyes follow Michael and the boy, and Buddy sees me watching them.

"Michael is a very good friend of the boy's mother," he explains.

I nod but wonder why he's telling me this. Can he see how uncomfortable I feel? Or how pissed I am at Michael for making me feel this discomfort?

Of course I won't say anything. It's not part of my job to speak up. I wear my perfect screenwriter's poker face, and whatever is thrown my way is fine with me. But the agoraphobic inside of me just wants to get out of there as quickly as possible. Escape is not an option, not at the moment. And

I am feeling as trapped here as I've ever felt outside of my house.

"He ate too much pizza!" Michael says, coming back into the living room. "Too many carbs make you sleepy," he laughs.

"My kids fall asleep all the time when I read to them," I say. But I have to admit I'm not happy my words have put the little boy to sleep. Or that the little boy was even there in the room to hear them.

"I like it," Buddy says, meaning my story. He says it like he's pleasantly surprised.

"It's so good!" Michael says with a smile.

Buddy looks at his watch. "Maybe we should wait to finish reading the rest of it. It's late."

"Do you want me to come back and read the last act?" I ask Michael. "Or should I just send you the pages?"

"Please come back and read!" Michael answers, excitedly. "I love it when you read to me!"

Buddy tells me that he'll coordinate his schedule with Stella, and she'll call me to set up a time for the next meeting.

Looks like Buddy is joining our team. It's not just Michael and me anymore.

And I'm not sure exactly what that means.

On the drive back home, my head was spinning.

I couldn't stop thinking about Michael and the young boy. I wanted to make sense of something that maybe I just didn't understand. I knew that Michael thought of himself as Peter, but what I had witnessed didn't make me think of *Peter Pan* at all. I couldn't picture Peter holding hands with one of the Lost Boys or sitting close to him, and wrapping the boy in his arms so lovingly.

It reminded me of something else.

Something I had heard years ago, but didn't want to believe.

A friend of mine worked in the office of a Hollywood music company. She had told me in confidence about the rumors of a "relationship" between Michael Jackson and one of the executives of the company. The man had been a mentor to Michael professionally, but he had also been much more. The office gossip was that the man had been molesting Michael since he was a young boy. It was on the down low, and people there kept it to themselves for fear of losing their jobs.

I thought the story my friend told me was cruel and malicious gossip. It reminded me of something a Broadway star once shared with me about becoming famous. She said she knew she had "made it" the morning she looked out her kitchen window, and saw some strangers going through her trash. Suddenly, people were interested in her.

"You know you've made it big when there are rumors about you," she had said. "Even if they're lies, it doesn't matter. People only talk about you when you get famous."

I just assumed that those rumors about Michael and the executive were part of a celebrity mystique. I never imagined that they could be true.

Until tonight.

If Michael had a relationship with a man when he was a young boy, maybe he doesn't think there's anything wrong with that kind of a bond. His closeness to the boy seemed easy and relaxed, and Michael looked comfortable being with him. Nothing about his behavior indicated that Michael thought what he was doing was problematic or anything less than normal. Maybe that's what made me feel so ill at ease. So concerned. So confused.

How does Hollywood not know about this?

If I've seen Michael cuddling a young boy and holding hands with him, who else has seen something like this? Or knows about it? Or maybe knows even more about it than I know. And doesn't Michael care? Doesn't he know what people might think, or how they might interpret his behavior? Michael may be pure of heart, childlike and innocent, but he's also 32 years old, and even the purest of intentions can be misunderstood.

I can't be the first person in this industry that has witnessed something like this about Michael. Or have I seen something tonight that hasn't been uncovered yet? Something that has been kept hidden: a secret known only to a few?

I know what it means to keep a secret.

Is this Michael's secret, just as agoraphobia is mine?

Did I see something he usually keeps private? And if I did, why was Michael showing this side of himself to me?

Or was I just being an overly dramatic screenwriter with a much too active imagination? Was my friend's story a true one, or just something made up by an office of bored secretaries?

I didn't know what the truth was.

I wasn't sure I wanted to find out.

23
It's Complicated

When you're in show business, and something serious happens that you're not sure how to handle, you do what everyone else in Hollywood does: You call your agent.

I call Raymond at his office early the next morning. His secretary isn't even in yet, but two things I know about Raymond: he goes to work early, and he can't resist a ringing telephone. It's not even 8 a.m. but he picks up anyway.

I want this phone call to be off the record.

"How did it go last night?" he asks nervously, knowing that I was scheduled to read the treatment to Michael, and that I wouldn't be calling so early unless there was a problem.

"You have to promise me you won't talk about what I'm about to tell you," I say to him seriously.

"He hated it! Did he hate it?!"

"Raymond, this is important. I don't want to talk about the script."

Now he knows this is serious.

"Tell me everything you know about Michael," I ask. "All the dirt."

If there were rumors about Michael and boys that he had befriended, Raymond would have heard them. Agents pride themselves in knowing the dirt about everyone in town. They're agents; it's part of their job to know people's vulnerabilities.

"He's weird!" Raymond says. "Everybody knows that. Why? What happened? What did he do?"

I tell Raymond everything. About the boy, and Michael cuddling with him on the couch. About how late it was, and there wasn't a parent in sight. I tell him that it really bothered me as a mother, that I'd shared photos of my own kids with Michael, that I was hoping they could meet him one day, and he'd invite them to Neverland. I said that I didn't understand what I had witnessed at the Hideaway, but I'd heard rumors about Michael as a boy, and now I wasn't so sure they were only rumors, and I never wanted Michael to ever meet my kids, and I ask Raymond if he's heard anything about Michael and young boys.

"No!" he tells me adamantly. "Nothing like *that*," he says, sounding totally shocked, and repulsed. "That's serious. That can kill a career!"

I know by Raymond's tone of voice that he's telling me the truth. If there was any gossip about Michael's involvement with children, Raymond would have heard all about it. Hollywood is too small of an industry town to keep that kind of secret quiet.

"You can't tell anyone about this," I say.

"Of course not!" he promises.

Not because it's the right thing to do.

"This could kill the project!"

Spoken like a true agent.

I tell him about Buddy sitting in on the meeting.

"What?! Who?!"

I give him Buddy's name and tell him he's a writer and producer.

"What the hell was he doing there?!" Raymond asks, indignantly. "Howard will have a stroke if he finds out that somebody else was at this meeting, and it wasn't him."

I wasn't going to tell Howard. The last thing Disney needed to know right now was that Michael was cuddling with a minor. I didn't want to be a whistleblower when I didn't know for sure what I was really blowing the whistle on.

"You need to turn in this treatment *now*!" he says to me urgently.

"I can't. The little boy fell asleep at the end of Act Two."

"What?!"

"I have to read the rest of the treatment to Michael."

"Oh my God, just give him the pages! He can read them himself!"

"He wants me to personally read them to him," I explain.

"Katzenberg is having a fit," Raymond finally admits. "I didn't want to tell you and make you more nervous. Howard's been holding him off, but he can't do it much longer. Jeffrey says you're working for Disney and not Michael. He's pissed!"

"I can't give Katzenberg pages before I read them to Michael. I promised I'd read them to him first, and he'll take it personally if I don't. I don't want to get on the wrong side of Michael," I explain.

"I'll handle Disney," Raymond promises. "I'll tell them the treatment's being typed up. You handle Michael. Get that next meeting and turn this puppy in!"

I call Stella right after lunch, and she seems eager to set up the next meeting. I brace myself, expecting a date no sooner than a month.

"Next Friday at 7," she says. "Michael can't wait to meet!" she tells me excitedly.

We only have to hold off Disney for a week. That won't be hard. I'll just tell them I'm sick, and I won't answer my phone.

I spend the next week making copies of the treatment, binding them with covers and practicing my reading out loud to my kids.

"Mommy, we already heard this!" my son protests, as I pull out my treatment once again at bedtime.

"Mommy needs to practice," I tell him. "Besides, it might help you sleep."

I am more than ready for this next meeting.

Stella calls me the night before we meet to cancel. There's no explanation except that Michael is busy. I am close to tears. I have no other choice than to confide in Stella, hoping she can help. I tell her that Disney is beyond angry: Katzenberg is fuming. They are pressing me to turn in the treatment.

"Oh honey, you can't do that," she says, concerned. "Michael will be so hurt." The words sound ominous. Subtext: A hurt Michael is not a happy Michael. And an unhappy Michael might just walk.

"Nobody wants to hurt Michael," I explain. "But the Disney executives keep telling me, 'We're paying your salary—not Michael.'"

Stella says she'll fax Michael at the recording studio and ask him if he wants me to turn in the pages or to come over to the Hideaway on Monday to read them in person. It's the best she can do, she tells me, so I agree. She calls me back within the hour to say that Michael will read the pages. All I have to do is drop them off at the Hideaway this weekend.

"Disney is being very rude," she admits to me, in her sternest voice. "This is a major, and important project. You don't treat Michael Jackson like this. And Michael is adamant: He doesn't want you to turn in anything until he's read these pages."

It means stalling over the weekend. But I've held off the studio already for a week, what's another two days? Three days counting Monday, when finally I'll be meeting with Michael.

Stella has told me to drop off the treatment at Michael's so we drive out to the Wilshire address after a family dinner on Friday night. The doorman brightens when he sees me and smiles at my two children in the backseat.

"Meeting Mr. Jackson tonight?" he asks.

"Not tonight," I say, handing him a manila envelope with the treatment inside of it. "But Michael's waiting to read this," I tell him. "Could you please make sure he gets it right away?"

"Soon as he gets in," he promises me, with a tip of his hat.

I try not to think about the project during the weekend. We keep busy with the kids, taking them to Knott's Berry Farm on Sunday. Later that night, I settle in to watch the previously taped Sammy Davis Jr. Tribute on television, waiting to watch Michael's performance in it. He sings a song that he wrote just for Sammy, a ballad honoring him as an entertainer. When the credits roll, I'm surprised to see that Buddy also wrote one of the songs performed on the show. But what happens next completely catches me off guard as a voice on the television suddenly makes an announcement.

"Michael Jackson hospitalized with chest pains! News at 11!"

I am shocked beyond words.

24
Time Is Running Out

Michael has been admitted to St. John's Hospital in Santa Monica. All that the news is reporting is that he was suffering chest pains, and they're keeping him overnight for observation.

I can't sleep at all that night. I wonder all sorts of things as I lay there, worrying. Did I push Michael too much? Did he feel pressured to read the treatment? On top of all of his other work, he's been meeting with me late at night; it's been long hours and lots of stress. Is he having heart problems, and if he is, what does this mean to the project?

I'm up before the kids the next morning, searching on television for any news about Michael's condition. I finally find a report that says he is suffering from exhaustion. It wasn't a heart attack as the press originally had suggested. It was pure exhaustion brought on by stress and too many long hours of work.

I saw how tired Michael was after all of his traveling and from the emotion of Ryan White's funeral. Maybe I should have insisted that we take a break or not meet so late at night. But Howard has been relentless about seeing a treatment. Why the big rush, I wonder? I have until the end of September to turn in a treatment. This is only June, so why the pressure? And why is Katzenberg suddenly pushing for pages?

I want to call Michael and see how he's feeling. But I know there's no way I can possibly get through all of his entourage to speak directly to him. I call Stella to ask how he's doing, and she says he's better, but really worn out. I tell her I'd like to send flowers, and she says he'll be in the hospital a few more days. I call a florist to order a tiny, delicate bonsai tree, something sweet and whimsical that I hope will cheer Michael up. I send it to him at St. John's with a note wishing him a speedy recovery, and I sign it fondly.

The studio is eerily quiet for the rest of the week, and there are no frantic phone calls from Howard. Maybe it's because Michael is in the hospital, and everyone is worried about his health. Or more honestly, the health of their project. But once Michael has been released from the hospital, Howard calls me first thing that morning.

"He's fine," he tells me, matter-of-factly. "He just pulled some ligaments in his ribcage."

"I'll call Stella today to see when Michael wants to meet…"

Howard interrupts me before I can finish.

"We've run out of time," he says, ominously.

I remind Howard about the September deadline in my contract. I tell him that I don't think Disney can afford to anger Michael just because they want to read the story treatment before he does.

"This isn't about Michael anymore," Howard says firmly.

"...What does that mean?" I ask.

"I can't get into it," he explains. "The studio wants to make this film happen, but we need the treatment right now—the future of the project depends on it."

I can't tell if Howard is being overly dramatic, or if Project M is about to crash and burn. I try to pump him for more information, but he tells me he can't leak anything at the moment. Once I turn in the treatment, then he'll be able to talk about it and give me all the details.

I call Raymond right away.

"Howard is being cryptic," I say. "What do you know?"

Raymond swears up and down that he doesn't know anything more than what Howard has just told me. But if Howard has hinted at a problem with the project, he's betting that something is up, and we definitely should be worried. He promises me that he'll ask around, and try to find out what exactly is going on.

What do I do in the meantime?

"You better turn in the treatment," he says nervously.

I spend the rest of the day trading phone calls with Stella. She's left me a message saying that Michael has been trying to reach me, and I try for hours to connect with him. But at the end of the day, the only person I'm able to get on the phone is Stella.

"Disney wants me to turn in the treatment," I tell her.

"When?"

"Right now."

"Oh, honey," she says with disappointment in her voice.

I feel just as disappointed.

Michael and I share a special bond. Nobody knows *Peter Pan* more than we do. Nobody loves Tink more than the two of us, or understands Wendy, and the Lost Boys, Hook, and all of the pirates. Characters to everyone else, but for Michael and me, they've become real, coming to us in the late nights we've shared, from the time we've spent together, and the love we have for Neverland and everything it represents: the innocence of childhood, the power of imagination, and the freedom that comes from letting go. Michael is the one person who really understands all of this. If it wasn't for him and this project, I'd still be hiding in the house. Without an office. Still too frightened to drive. And with no sense of real freedom in my life. I've learned how to fly again thanks to Michael, and *Peter Pan*. For everything I've accomplished, and for all of the work that we've done together, I owe Michael a second chance.

"One more meeting," I tell Stella. "And then I have to turn the story in."

I hope Michael is ready.

25
One More Meeting

Michael is alone when I show up at the Hideaway at 9:30 p.m. He looks good and rested. There's no sign of the matching fedoras or the little boy from New Zealand. More importantly, there's no sign of Buddy. It's just the two of us again, and that seems only right on a night when I will be reading the rest of the story treatment to him.

"How are you?" I ask with concern.

"Oh, I'm fine," he says. "I'm better now. A little sore, but not much."

"I was really worried about you," I tell him. I say it sincerely because I mean it. Michael and I have connected over the last few months; maybe it's not friendship exactly, but there's a closeness that happens when people in show business work intensely with one another. Jobs don't last long in this business, so we make up in feelings what we don't have in time.

"I'm fine," he says softly, a little uncomfortable by the attention.

I can see his shyness again and feel him retreating.

"I sent you a little bonsai tree," I say.

"You did?" he says, his eyes widening.

"It reminded me of Tinkerbell."

He smiles, liking the connection.

"I thought it might cheer you up."

"It sounds sweet," he says.

"You didn't see it?" I ask, not understanding. "I sent it to you at St. John's."

"All the flowers and gifts I get are sent over to the Children's Hospital," he explains. "There are always so many of them, so many flowers, and lots of stuffed animals. The children love getting them! But I never see them," he says.

I nod, a little bit hurt. He never even saw the bonsai tree I sent him.

"But thank you," he adds, quietly. Politely.

Michael lives in such a different world than I do. It's naïve of me not to remember that and useless to ever try looking for a way to bridge that difference.

The doorbell rings, and it's Buddy. He apologizes for being late, and the tone changes in the room as he takes a seat. It's all business now, and Michael looks relieved that he's finally there. I recognize the unspoken cue for the meeting to begin, and so I pull out my story, turning to the pages I haven't shared with them yet.

"Did you have a chance to read the whole treatment?" I ask Michael.

"I think Michael wanted to wait until you could read it to us," Buddy explains with a smile, answering for him.

I glance over at Michael, but if I'm seeking confirmation or camaraderie, I won't find it with him. He has retreated without leaving the room; he seems content to allow Buddy to run the meeting. There is no hiding from this except in the pages of my story. So, slowly I ease into them, welcoming their reality over the reality in this room.

It is a scene-by-scene breakdown, a film laid out in black and white, with words on pages, creating images in the mind and not on the screen. As I speak, the room fills with action and pathos: the pirates search for fairy dust treasure, and Tinkerbell is killed by Hook; the children are captured, and Peter's battle with Hook rages; good triumphs over evil; Tinkerbell is reborn, and the faeries return victoriously; Neverland is saved, and Peter sails Hook's ship through magic waterfalls, back into the world.

"'Peter looks over at the Lost Boys, wanting desperately to ask them to stay,'" I read from the pages. "But they are gathered at the bow of the ship, their eager eyes on the approaching waterfall, already curious about the adventures waiting for them beyond, in the real world. And Peter knows just by watching them that their stay with him is over: he has to let them go.'"

This time while reading I stay grounded in the words, never taking flight above the room to watch Buddy or Michael. Instead, I am swept away by Peter, flying high above the beauty of Neverland. Safe within the certainty of the story and free to feel all of the feelings of the words: the sadness, the loss, the joy, and at the ending, happiness to be able to come back home again, better and richer for having had the journey.

When I finish reading, the room is quiet. What it means, I don't know. But I'm grateful for the silence because a part of me is adjusting to my return. Leaving Neverland is never easy.

"Very good," Buddy finally says.

"It's wonderful, Darlene," Michael adds softly.

These words should be enough, but of course they're not. Buddy begins to ask questions, and Michael simply sits back and says nothing. Everything we've worked on together, talked about, and considered is now under Buddy's microscope. He picks away at a character trait here, a story point there, grabbing at threads and pulling apart what has taken months to weave together. If he were Michael, I'd be taking notes. If he were Steven, I'd be listening. I would make changes; I'd shape the story in the direction they wanted to go. But he's not Michael or Steven, and so I pretend to take notes, and I nod conciliatorily, just to keep the peace. Pulling inside of myself emotionally, I simply retreat. When an appropriate amount of time has passed, and I've fielded as many of Buddy's questions that I can tolerate, I bring the meeting to an abrupt halt.

"Disney wants to read this," I say.

"Michael thinks he'd like to read it one more time before you turn it in."

I look over at Michael, not wanting to hear how he feels, or what he thinks as answers from Buddy, but from Michael himself. He has trouble looking at me, and that says more to me than words.

I've done everything in my power to keep Michael 100% happy. I've been the perfect little screenwriter: I have nurtured, encouraged, coaxed, and enticed. We've been playmates together, sucking Jolly Roger candies and giggling over nonsense. But that's over now. We've stopped being kids.

Well, I've stopped at least.

Michael seems content staying just the way he is. He likes having people speak for him. Running his life. Handling his affairs. Ordering his pizzas and making excuses for him. If not Stella, then Buddy. Or his lawyer, his manager, or anyone willing to run interference. It's easy to find people willing to run your life for you. All you have to do is allow it and pay the bills. And maybe throw a fit every now and then when you disagree. But then, there's no such thing as disagreeing with you because in the end you always get the yes. Yes to whatever you want. Whether it's using drugs or surrounding yourself with children who don't really belong there. You may seek counsel, but no one's advice overrides what you really want to do. So you always get your way.

Always.

And isn't that just like being a kid?

Now that I was a fully formed grown-up in this relationship, I resented having to deal with Michael, the child. I wanted him to match me as an equal, not just with ideas but as a person too. I was doing all this grown-up hard work, fighting panic attacks, overcoming anxiety, and just trying to drive two and a half goddamn blocks. All of those eccentricities and rough edges we sometimes have as people, intensified perhaps in the arts, take hard work as adults to overcome. I was doing the heavy lifting, and I wanted Michael to be doing it too. I didn't want to have to figure out why these children were in his life, and why he wasn't doing something to stop it. I didn't want to have to go through roadblocks to reach him as a person. I wanted us to be equals. But he was Michael Jackson, and he didn't have to do anything he didn't want to do.

Buddy had already told me that Michael wanted to read the treatment one more time before turning it into the studio. Why should I need to hear the words from Michael himself?

But I do need to hear them.

I'm not moving from the couch. I'm not reaching for my workbag or gathering up my notes to leave. I still remain seated, waiting until I hear the words directly from Michael.

He owes me that.

When our eyes finally lock, he knows that he does.

"I want another meeting before you turn it in," he says, simply.

I've seen this look in Michael's eyes before, and I know not to push it. It's the way he looked at Martin, his housekeeper. And I know if I stay a moment longer, the steel-cold tone of voice he used with Martin he'll use with me too. I'm just another employee. And he's the boss.

I know better than to resist.

I also know what I need to do next.

26
A Surprise Ending

I notify the messenger service first thing in the morning. I call Howard's office and leave word with his secretary.

"Please tell him he'll have the *Peter Pan* treatment by noon."

I call Stella and explain to her that I'm turning it in.

"That's too bad, honey. Disney's put you in a rough position."

I tell her I'll be happy to meet with Michael once we hear from the studio. We can get together and work out any ideas he has, and if he wants to call me, he can. I'm available if Michael wants to talk to me, I tell Stella. Please let him know that.

Raymond calls after lunch and says that the studio is thrilled to have the pages, and the treatment is being put on the weekend read for Katzenberg.

I get a phone call from Howard on Monday morning.

"It's wonderful!" he says in a voice that really does sound appreciative, and genuine. "You've done some wonderful, really creative things. It's terrific!" he gushes again.

My heart flips with hope.

"I wish we could make it," he says awkwardly.

There's always a "But…" in Hollywood. You just have to wade through the bullshit long enough to find it.

"What did you say?" I ask, knowing full well what he said, but not understanding the enthusiasm with which he's said it.

"We can't make it."

"Could you be a little more specific," I ask. "You can't make *this* story. But you could make another?"

"We can't do *Peter Pan*," he admits. "At all. Not at all."

"Is it because of Michael?" I ask, wondering if I've angered him by turning in the treatment. Has he pulled out of the project?

"Michael has nothing to do with the decision. He loves *Peter Pan*; you know that. He's dying to play Peter."

"So you love the story, and Michael's still onboard?"

"It's Steven," he admits quietly.

I get a chill up my spine.

"He didn't like it?" I ask, through gritted teeth.

What follows next is every screenwriter's nightmare.

"He's got another script," Howard says, with the words sticking in his throat.

"Another script?"

"It's called *Hook*."

I can only guess what it's about, and I'm sure that Howard must be explaining the plot to me because he's still talking at the other end of the phone, but I can't hear him. I haven't heard anything since he said the word: Hook. Besides, I don't really need anyone to explain to me why a script called *Hook* might kill a *Peter Pan* project.

"This is an already written, ready to go script?!" I ask Howard, as I slowly come out of my shock-induced mental paralysis. "And Steven just *happened* to stumble over it?"

"Somebody just sent it to him."

"Yeah, right!"

"Swear to God, Darlene. Steven didn't have this in development when we all had lunch together. This just dropped into his lap. It's just timing, terrible, terrible timing. Don't take this personally."

"So that's it for *Peter Pan*? That's a wrap?"

"We love what you did!" he says in a voice that's way too enthusiastic for the news it's bringing. "Jeffrey loved it!"

I suddenly understand the enthusiasm: Howard gets points for one of his writers doing well. If you wade out into the bullshit far enough, you always find the truth.

Unless you drown before getting to it.

"Maybe in a few years," Howard says, ever the optimist. "After *Hook* is made. Maybe we can revisit this."

Bullshit. All bullshit. Steven Spielberg doesn't do things twice. Howard knows this, I know this, and even first year film students know this. But what's Howard supposed to say? He's only the messenger. At least he called me personally, something the director didn't do. How long could it have taken for Steven to pick up the phone? To say to the screenwriter,

"Sorry, this didn't work out." And honestly, it would've been a kind gesture if he had. But this is Hollywood, and nobody says you have to be kind.

At least not to the screenwriter.

Don't cry, I tell myself, as my eyes begin to well up. At least don't cry with Howard on the phone. Say goodbye and then you can cry all you want.

"Goodbye, Howard," I say to him quickly, hoping he can't hear the tremble in my voice.

"Don't feel bad, Darlene!" he says.

"No, I feel great! Thanks, Howard!"

I'm hoping he hung up before my first sob.

27
Fade Out

Every project begins with the highest of hopes, and goes downhill from there. But what people outside the industry don't know is that most films flounder and fail in the development stage, like Michael's *Peter Pan*, before they ever have a chance of flopping on the screen. There's absolutely nothing a screenwriter can do about it.

It's called "Development Hell."

I had my first taste of it several years ago when I was hired to write the sequel to a prestigious Emmy winning CBS television film. My deal was freshly closed, I was sent off to research the story in Washington D.C., and when I returned I had my first meeting at the production offices in Studio City. I ran into the president of the production company who was hanging out in the coffee room, looking bored, as he tossed popcorn in the air. A portly, middle-aged gentleman with rolled up sleeves, wearing polyester slacks and sporting a Bronx accent, he seemed more like the owner of a trucking firm than a well respected television mogul.

"Whadaya workin' on?" he asked me, tossing a kernel of corn high in the air and just missing it with his mouth.

I told him the name of the project, saying it proudly. It was my first official movie of the week.

"Oh yeah!" he said, brightening at the project title. "It'll never get made," he added, nonchalantly reaching for another handful of corn.

"Excuse me?" I asked, certain I had misheard him.

"Don't worry," he assured me. "You'll get paid; you'll do a great job; it'll get you more work."

"But if I write a great script, they'll *have* to make it!" I said, sounding just like Judy Garland in every MGM film I'd ever seen.

The producer just laughed, having seen those same movies himself.

"It'll never happen, kid." he said with a friendly, fatherly pat on my shoulder, and disappearing into his office, leaving a trail of crushed popcorn (and my dreams) in his wake.

I did two drafts and a polish before CBS killed that project.

But the producer was right: I got paid, and I was hired for more films. No harm, no foul. Except it still hurt. A lot. Because the truth is you don't just write for the money. It's painful when something you've created, something you've invited into your life, which in fact, has taken over your life, simply goes away, and never has a reality of its own.

It never crossed my mind that *Peter Pan* starring Michael Jackson, directed by Steven Spielberg would never reach the silver screen. There's this blind faith you latch onto when you become a screenwriter. Or maybe it's just some kind of delusional madness that comes along with the trade. Looking back, I now see the flaws and the improbabilities of the project. But in the summer of 1990, just a few months after *Peter Pan* fell apart, all I could think of was how unfair it was that the *Hook* sets of the Jolly Roger and the backdrops of Neverland were being built only eight miles from my house. And the script that gave birth to those sets was not from my keyboard but from someone else's.

As badly as I felt as the screenwriter, my heart really went out to Michael. His whole life was centered on his Peter Pan identity, and it was always his dream to play out that role on film. It must have been devastating for him and humiliating also to have the role taken away from him. Instead of Michael's *Peter Pan*, it would be Robin Williams who was cast in the role. And I think that must have hurt Michael deeply.

As soon as I found out about *Hook* and Steven's involvement with the project, I knew that there would never be a chance that a Spielberg *Peter Pan* starring Michael Jackson would ever happen. I remembered Michael's words, his concern about the director not having enough "heart," and it all seemed so prophetic. I wondered how long Steven had known about the *Hook* script, or how many meetings Michael and I kept having while he knew? I was just the screenwriter: the bottom of the food chain. But Michael was a star, and I thought he would have been treated better.

I immediately wrote a note to Michael, telling him how badly I felt about the timing of the *Hook* project, and Steven's involvement with it. I said that I hoped someday he'd get the chance to play the role of Peter, a role I felt he was destined to play. I told him that I loved working with him, and I hoped some day in the future we could work together again. I took a cab out to the Hideaway that same night, and I left the note with the doorman.

I never got a reply.

I never heard from Michael again.

The rumor around town that summer was that Steven had offered Michael a small role as one of the pirates. An extra's role with no lines, it was only one day of work, but it was a chance to dress up in costume, and to play on the gigantic Jolly Roger set on the Burbank Studios lot. It was something a 3rd grader would love: playing pirates with all of the boys. I don't know for sure if Michael took the role or not.

I hope in my heart that he didn't.

Postscript

Howard was telling me the truth when he said the studio was happy with my work: Disney rewarded me with back-to-back double blind script deals. Raymond was ecstatic to negotiate the contract, even when I told him I only wanted to write three and not four Disney scripts.

And no animation.

Raymond had earned his stripes as an agent. More importantly, he did one of the kindest things anyone in Hollywood has ever done for a screenwriter. After the project fell apart, he showed up at my house with a little wrapped gift. Inside, was a tiny Peter Pan clay figurine—the kind you buy as a souvenir at Disneyland. But this one was special, or at least it was to me. It hadn't been painted, and the clay had never been fired in a kiln: It was an unfinished Peter Pan. And to me it was the most beautiful of any I had ever seen. Raymond proved to me that there *are* good people in Hollywood, and that sometimes they are capable of doing kind things.

I'd be lying to you if I said everything was fine after Project M fell apart. It's true: I had screenplays to write, so it didn't hurt my career. Failure is looked on as an accomplishment in Hollywood. Although the film had fallen apart, the good news was I had worked on a huge "A-List" film project, and I hadn't been fired from it. It was great PR, and Raymond was thrilled that he could finally talk about it around town.

But no matter how many script assignments they might send your way, you're always left with the hurt from the one that never got made. This time, the hurt was big. All of the stress from the last seven months hit me hard, and I came down with a nasty case of chronic fatigue syndrome. An interesting illness because it makes you feel like you've been run over by a large train, and there's no way possible you can leave the house. Literally. You have trouble getting out of bed, much less going through your front door. Such an ironic illness to lay low an agoraphobic.

It took me six months, but I did get better.

Just in time to watch the *Hook* commercials on television.

Of course the film was a blockbuster success, and that was hard to accept. But most of the critics hated it, and I found much comfort in that. Sour grapes? Absolutely. They never tasted better.

But the big news was that David decided he wanted to be a teacher.

So with the Disney deal in my back pocket we packed up our life and moved away from Hollywood, heading to another city two hours away. David went to graduate school to get an M.A., and he became a high school English/Performing Arts teacher. A damn good one too.

And I started to drive again.

Slowly.

One block at a time.

To school to pick up the kids. To practices, and doctor appointments, Little League Games, gymnastics, and coffee with my friends.

Nowadays I'm working on freeway driving.

I can only go a few exits before I get too nervous, a little panicky, and my eyes frantically start searching for the next off ramp. Driving to Hollywood two hours away is definitely out of the question. But Raymond makes sure that a Town Car and driver are part of my contract and getting to meetings is never a problem I have to worry about.

I think of Michael every time a driver holds open a door for me. And I remind myself not to get used to it. Not to think that I deserve it or that it defines my life or who I am.

On days when I'm writing, I like to drive by myself to the local lake.

Nestled in the middle of a nearby neighborhood, you can't see the lake at first. You walk down an old, forgotten road, and when you come to the end, the lake is waiting there as your reward. There's a bench I sit on, perched on the shore, and across from me I see the sprawling foothills—the other side of the Santa Ynez Mountains. Just below me is the lake, filled with egrets, Great Blue Herons, Mallard ducks, and a swan or two. In the center of the water sits a small island that is lush, and beautiful. No one is allowed to swim or use boats here, so it's unreachable. It always reminds me of Neverland: remote and only accessible by those few willing to break the rules to get there any way they can.

I sit at the edge of the water, gazing out at that island, like Wendy, knowing that Neverland is a place I once visited but no longer yearn to reach. The island doesn't have a pull on me anymore. It's enough just to see it at a distance, reveling in its beauty and remembering a time when I would have done anything to get there.

But not anymore.

What matters the most to me now is knowing that I am able to get to this place on my own. With my car parked down the road and with me as the driver.

Growing up isn't so bad after all.

Darlene Craviotto

AN AGORAPHOBIC'S GUIDE TO HOLLYWOOD

How Michael Jackson Got Me Out of the House

Darlene Craviotto has worked professionally in the entertainment industry for over twenty-five years. She wrote Hallmark Hall of Fame's *Love Is Never Silent,* which won an *Emmy* for Outstanding Television Movie. Her feature film, *Squanto: A Warrior's Tale,* a Walt Disney Film, garnered a Teddy Award for Best Family Film. Her award-winning play, *Pizza Man,* has been performed all over the world. Ms. Craviotto is married, has two children, and lives in Santa Barbara, California.

Made in the USA
San Bernardino, CA
06 January 2018